Flying Colors

Sarah Moore

© 2015 Copyright
By Branden Books

Library of Congress Cataloging-in-Publication Data

Moore, Sarah, 1980-
 Flying colors : the biography of Victor Tatelman / by Sarah Moore. -- 1st edition.
   pages cm
 Includes bibliographical references and index.
  ISBN 978-0-8283-2573-8 (pbk. : alk. paper) -- ISBN 978-0-8283-2575-2 (e-book : alk. paper) 1. Tatelman, Victor. 2. United States. Army Air Forces. Bombardment Group, 345th. Bombardment Squadron, 499th. 3. Bomber pilots--United States--Biography. 4. Mitchell (Bomber) 5. World War, 1939-1945--Aerial operations, American. 6. World War, 1939-1945--Pacific Area. I. Title.

 D790.263499th .M66 2015
 940.54'4973092--dc23
 [B]

                                       2015015722

ISBN 9780828325738 Paperback
ISBN 9780828325752 E-Book

Branden Books
PO Box 812084, Wellesley MA 02482

www.brandenbooks.com

Sarah Moore, *Flying Colors*

*Thank you
 & happy reading,
 Sarah Moore*

Acknowledgements

This book would not have seen the light of day if not for the support and encouragement of many people. I would like to say thank you to each person who has influenced this project and helped me on my way in writing it. My partner and love, Drew Moore, has put up with countless bouts of self doubt and random outbursts of inspiration. Without his patience, support, and loving encouragement I never would have found the courage to even take up this project. Kathryn Miles, who read early drafts and offered insight on every angle helped me to find the shape and breadth of this book. Gretchen Legler, helped me to collect random ideas and scattered essays into something cohesive. Lynda Moore spent untold hours combing through old photo albums, file folders stuffed full of memories and official records. She collected them, and sent them on with a frenzied passion that kept this project going. Most importantly, Vic, thank you for spending days with me in person, on the phone, over email, and through the mail recounting your stories and taking the time to share your perspective. This book is yours as much as it is mine. Thank you.

Table of Contents

Introduction 6
Getting There 7
Primary Flight School 11
Pearl Harbor 15
Murphy 18
Precision and Advanced Training 23
First Assignments 28
Dirty Dora 36
Biscuit Bombs & Barges 38
Laundry Duty 42
Shot Down 45
Photo Op 48
Wewak 51
Ropopo 53
Prices Paid 58
Shot 59
Kavieng 62
The Nose Gun 66
Olive 71
Yalau 93
Never Volunteer 96
Life at ADVON 102
Dirty Dora II 108
The General's Plane 115
First Radar Countermeasures 118
The Tank and Barn 124
Home Building 126
Destroying a Destroyer 128
End of Hostilities 131
The Surrender 137
Vacation in Seoul 143
Stranded 148
Reflections after the War 154

Introduction

Vic's voice pours through the cell phone in my hand, deep and growling. It's how I imagine an engine of a B-25 bomber, the kind he flew during the war, would have sounded. His love of the machines is so deep and full that over the years he eventually came to sound as one of them. His is the voice of one familiar with order and a chain of command, a rough riding combat pilot with keen intelligence and a fierce eye for incongruities. His syllables are delivered punctually with a no nonsense clarity. No time is wasted on unnecessary communication or frivolity.

Reaching across the distance, even cell phone reception is respectful, or fearful, to defy the precision demanded by his military articulation. The man, who is now in his nineties and a concise communicator, is also a lover of story-telling. I asked him to share some of his stories with me; what I came to learn surprised me. I came to understand more fully how world views, over generations, have been shaped and influenced. His story filled in the blank spaces I encountered history books with faces and intimate tales of loss and love. World War II reached over the distance of time and grasped my hand in order to make me pay attention.

Getting There

On October 14, 1941, Victor Tatelman became a soldier in the United States Army Air Corps. In the photo of his military id, Vic's dark hair is combed back from his high forehead. Though not religious, his features hint at a Jewish heritage: Strong dark eyebrows, a prominent nose, and deep eyes. His gaze is off and to the right, as though he were catching a glimpse of the promise his future held. His lips are soft, almost smirking. His face is slender and set above narrow uniformed shoulders. His slenderness is offset by the confidence in his expression. Expectant, as though he already knows the danger he will face; but finds it amusing. His is a face that a young woman would have found attractive, especially when he wore a uniform.

The first night he bed down in a military barracks, perhaps due to naivety and the enthusiasm of youth, Vic and his peers envisioned countless hours of flight, glory, exotic girls and adventure. The threats of death, injury and loss were only faintly acknowledged as vague risks rather than true potentialities.

The long gray barracks were full of the excited voices of young men, some just past puberty. Bags dumped on the floor, beds full and weighted down with pride, hope, and that exuberance that comes in the company of youth. Cigarette smoke coiled up to the ceiling, the insignia of comradeship and celebration at having made it this far. Underneath the cauliflower shaped smoke plumes groups of young men bunched together in two's and three's. They gestured with their hands, making small circles to emphasize points as they spoke. In the back corner was a gray metal desk with a small glass shaded lamp in the upper corner and one locking drawer stretched along the underside. A wooden chair faced the desk while the young man seated in it faced the room. Vic watched a game of cards that had spread out on one of the bunks, cigarettes were being wagered.

The room vibrated with the sound of men's voices, the clump of boots, and bed springs straining from too many bodies pressed on them. There rose a single command: "Attention!" The men snapped up, some gave awkward salutes. The recruits were instructed to form two lines for inspection. No uniforms had yet been issued and bags were still on the floor spilling contents under beds and underfoot. A uniformed officer paced slowly down the ranks, to eye each of his newest recruits, and to inform them of barracks protocol. This was the last time so much as a single boot would have been found out of place or off a foot.

After inspection the sergeant told the men that they would be assigned to training facilities across the country. The following morning they would be given those assignments and board trains for their respective destinations. The men were ordered to rest up and be ready to ship out in the morning. Then the sergeant turned his back and strode from the barracks as suddenly as he had entered, leaving the recruits to wonder where their journeys were about to lead them.

The men's conversation, after the sergeants' exit, revolved around the future and lasted late into the evening, well past lights out. Lying on hard cots, under stiff military blankets, Vic felt understanding creep in as stealthy as the cool fall air after dusk. Still awaiting uniforms and assignments, attempting to sleep in their underwear in a room full of near strangers; the men felt the first pangs of enlistment and the first hesitations of doubt. How long would they be in training? Then where would they be sent? What would training be like? How hard? How long? Would the war wait? Did they really want to go?

On the train the following morning, there were dozens of recruits from across Indiana. They were bound, like Vic, for Primary Flight Training School at Visalia, California. The Pullman cars were loaded down with these men. Each young face blending in with the next, equally matched with excitement, pride, and expectancy.

The two best words that would describe the trip are long and boring. The men distracted themselves with card games, reading, or spending as much time as possible sleeping their way through Middle America, that vast expanse of farmland with open sky and little else. Mile after mile of green cropland sped passed the windows of the Pullman cars. Fields of gold wheat, blending into endless rows of corn stalks tipped with silken heads. Border fences of barbed wire containing herds of grazing cattle that dotted the landscape whisked by like stop motion photography.

The young men were oblivious to the scenes of bounty that raced passed them. Instead they hunched over fists full of cards and trained their gazes away from the windows. They were each escaping for more exotic places, trading the aroma of pasture for that of gun oil and smoke. They had all left their respective worlds of expansive farming landscapes, quaint townships, and high school sweethearts.

A few who slept in the corners with their foreheads wobbling on the glass, were dreaming of the sweet faces that waved goodbye to them as they had boarded trains full up with other hopeful young men. The smell of engine smoke, meat sandwiches, and crumpled dirty laundry blended together in a strange perfume that seemed to cling. It was the smell of adventure, and they welcomed it the same way they were to welcome their first combat assignments.

Each day the trains stopped, morning and afternoon, at different towns. The men were ordered by uniformed officers to get off and form lines for exercise. The stretch of limbs pulled them out of their stupors and the slight regimen prepared them, in part, for what waited at the end of the line. Fifteen minutes each morning and afternoon saw dozens of young men, jumping, bending, reaching, and running in place, responding to the called out orders of a few confident superiors. All lined up under the sun, stretching and flexing in unison, they resembled the silk headed rows of corn that had swayed in the wind and passed by the windows of the preceding days.

Forced to exist for days on end in close quarters, sharing meals, exercise and card games, the men became friends and found similarities in their stories. One grew up on a farm in Ohio and had been to Cincinnati once when he was younger. Another had come from Chicago and had an uncle who ran a slaughter house. Many came from homes similar to Vic's, happy families living in small neighborhoods and small towns. A few, like Vic, were Jewish. Many were Catholic--some practicing and others not so much. Others still, agnostic. Their education was similar, high school, college with focuses in engineering and math. Some of the men had finished college and earned degrees. Others were like Vic and had enlisted as soon as they met the base requirements of two years college experience.

    They had all answered the same call, responded to the same yearnings. They wanted to fly the best planes, air combat training, fight the good fight, honor, glory, adventure. Many different paths had lead many different men to this very same train. Their fates were fixed and focused in the same direction. This shared path bound these men together and formed bonds of friendship and brotherhood that in many cases lasted lifetimes, some were to be cut drastically short.

Primary Flight School:

Because of his previous flying and CPTP (Civilian Pilot Training Program) experience, primary training was a breeze for Vic. The only real difference between the programs was the rankings. Visalia was like most army primary schools in the country in that it was civilian operated and incorporated civilian instructors. The only military personnel were the Commander of Cadets (a 1st Lieutenant) and the Director of Flying (a 2nd Lieutenant).

Shortly after arriving at Visalia, Vic was approached by the base commander. When the base commander wants to see someone, it's usually for an infringement, so naturally Vic was a bit concerned. Much to his surprise it was not neglect of the rules that had caught the Commanders attention, but Vic's high scores in his math and science courses in college. The Commander had a proposition.

There Vic stood, rigid and respectful before the base commander's desk in an unobtrusive white walled office with a book shelf in one corner housing binders and protocol manuals. There was a small pile of loose papers, still needing attention, resting in the upper right corner of the desk. The Base Commander sat on the powerful side looking up at Vic with a comfortable expression.

"Your record says you scored high in mathematics in your entrance exams."

Vic didn't respond, he wasn't asked a question. Instead he continued to hold attention and waited for the commander to finish. The commander smiled as he raised his head from the file containing Vic's scores. There was a joke in that smile, but also a suggestion of opportunity.

"Would you be able to handle a few trig problems for us?"

Vic was confused about what math problems had to do his being summoned. He didn't hesitate though and responded that he'd be happy to take a look at whatever it was the commander had. He hoped he could be of some service. It was an odd encounter and the only thing he could assume, since trigonometry was used extensively in surveying, the question must have something to do with a survey issue. The commander slapped the desktop lightly with the papers he had been holding and laugh-barked one word, "Good."

The light from the window cast geometric shadows on the floor. The math classes Vic had taken during high school and college had served him so well that he could have calculated the precise angle of the sun, light to dark ratios and trajectories from those shadows. It was for just that reason, the commander went on to explain, that Vic was to be appointed the trigonometry instructor during the remainder of his time on base. His peers in flight school were to be his pupils in ground school. He was shocked and a little uncertain, but accepted.

"Yes sir."

Vic was not given text books and was forced to write the curriculum from memory. A portable blackboard was borrowed from a public school nearby and set up in front of a dozen or so metal folding chairs that would serve as his students' desks. He taught algebra, geometry, and elementary trigonometry. Having just finished his own schooling Vic was fortunate enough that most of the concepts were freshly embedded in his mind and the basics were all he required mastery of from his pupils.

It made a funny sight, a room full of strong and energetic young men training for combat flying hunched over notebooks, struggling over the math problems they thought they had finished with in high school. Vic stood up at the front of the classroom, his uniform and dark hair dusted by chalk, explaining the principles of geometry, of sine and tangent, and simple angles. At the end of his course he saw to it that all of his students passed the final exam.

It was hard for him to believe that some of those kids, that was how he saw them, who had passed the written exam for the appointment to flight school, were just so dumb in basic algebra and geometry. Vic, still developing his patience, found himself tested in ways he had not anticipated. He had been expecting long tiresome hours in the cockpit learning advanced targeting systems and formation flying. Instead, he was elevated in those classroom hours from fellow cadet and drinking buddy to the role of teacher. It was a role that resulted in strung out patience and frazzled nerves. It took considerable effort to muscle past exasperation and explain basic mathematic principles again and again. Fine pilots all, but not so much as mathematicians.

In the CPTP, which Vic had completed before enlisting, he had flown Ryan PT-22s. In the Army Air Corps, the Waco UPF-7 was used. These bi-wing planes were piloted from the rear seat. They were highly agile and perfect for training future fighter pilots. Vic's ability in the plane quickly earned respect from both his fellow cadets and instructors. One incident in particular merited a Commendation.

Just after take-off, at about 100 feet, the Kinner engine of the plane stopped cold. Vic had spent weeks training for just such an eventuality. He knew that in the case of engine failure on take-off or below 200 feet to land straight ahead and to keep the nose down slightly to maintain flying speed. Avoiding, of course, obstacles in the glide path by utilizing small, gentle and coordinated turns. The touch-down should be approached with a gradual coasting.

At 100 ft Vic was in full thrill of take off. His back pressed into the seat and the wings of the plane dipping to one side then the other as the air pressure outside the plane pushed against his climb. The climb was steady and the ground dropped away when, without warning, the growling of the engine cut out and the props jerked to a stop. The tops of the buildings and trees that had been growing smaller beneath the body of the plane paused then began coming closer. The sky started to drift away.

Seated in the cockpit, the only indication on his face that might hint things were not going as planned would have been the pinch of his eyebrows over the bridge of his nose and a slight grimace on his lips. His gaze was aimed at the grove of orange trees, so too was the nose of the plane. Vic handled the controls as delicately as he would a woman. He aligned the body of his plane directly above the orchard below him. His descent was a smooth and gradual glide, aimed between two rows of trees.

Vic's attention was on the nose of the plane and where it was headed, so he hadn't seen the farmers' faded red pickup truck bouncing along, heedless of the parts that threatened to dislodge in the driver's haste. Nor did he see the emergency response vehicle racing from the flight line where Vic had taken off only moments before. What he saw was the open space between the orchard rows rushing closer at amazing speed.

The grass zipping past was still a few feet below the plane when the wings made contact with the first of the trees. Vic grunted at the force of the impact and grit his teeth in an effort to will the remains of the plane from spinning into a worse collision. Metal screamed and cables ripped when the wings of the plane were torn off. The carnage of the wreck was strewn behind the still racing plane body like amputated limbs bleeding control wires and fuel lines. The orchard suffered broken limbs and snapped trunks. The trees stood like wounded soldiers on either side of a gash cut into the earth by the downed plane.

The emergency response team arrived at the scene almost immediately, along with the grove owner. Everyone buzzed around in alarm. Medics clustered around him checking abrasions, pupils and heart rate. They urged immediate hospitalization but Vic refused, and received a lecture for doing so later. Instead he climbed into the front seat of the medical truck and demanded a ride back to the flight line for another go. A commendation letter from the Flight Deputy Commander went into his file, and a scrap of the fabric from the rudder of the plane went into Vic's duffle as a keepsake and reminder. The proud and young man that walked away from that first crash landing reclined in the front seat he had claimed. He had gotten a taste of the danger he would face later and liked it.

Pearl Harbor

Each generation is inevitably bound together in a single unifying tragedy, an act of war, terrorism, or cataclysmic natural disaster. For Vic's generation, Pearl Harbor was the day and event that altered world perspectives and established patriotic identities. The war was in Europe. America was still officially outside the conflict. Relying on Japanese embargoes, the Lend Lease Act, and the Neutrality act as a way of remaining outside the conflict. There were heated debates in Congress over Non-intervention in the "war without limits" that threatened to spread the world over. Japanese officials made threats of aggression toward the United States if embargoes were not lifted, or more troops sent to China. Germany was closing in on Stalin and made predictions to have seized control of Russia within a year. England, France, Italy, Germany, Russia, indeed, all of Europe was embroiled in the war and America was being drawn in without the consent of its people.

The younger generation of the time was confident in the power of America. While politicians debated over the inevitability and sensibility of entering into the war more directly, the young men of the nation were enlisting en masse. The naive excitement of young men across the nation to go to war was romanticized by an idea of a noble purpose, glory, and medals. One thought of uniforms and the feeling of European soil under thick boots. The smell of tank engines and French girl's perfume mingled in imaginations. Then Pearl Harbor happened.

On December 7, 1941 noon mess at the training facility in Visalia, CA was interrupted. Lunch was served in a crowded cafeteria teeming with cadets and food workers. Men in uniform carried trays with globs of mashed potatoes and chicken cutlets, both covered over with gelatinous gravy. Little paper cups of ice cream dotted table tops, special treats the men afforded themselves from time to time. Voices rolled through the air, confident and proud, before bouncing back off the cinder block walls. Vic was telling a joke but he was interrupted by an authoritative voice that punched through the commotion. The room went silent at the order to assemble.

The cadets stood in formation on the parade ground as they were informed of Japan's attack on Pearl Harbor and declaration of war. Shock and anger flowed through the men in a wave. No one had expected it and the blow came like a sucker punch to the cadets who vowed patriotic retribution. Romantic images of the honorable war cracked giving way to vengeful impulses. Inhuman beasts replaced caricatures of civilized soldiers in funny blue uniforms. It was to become a defining day that carried with it a heaviness that refused to be set down even decades later.

The commander of the base informed the assembly that Pearl Harbor had been attacked by air. The damage and number of casualties was still being determined. There were reports of parachutes being seen over the bay and of dive bombers flying in over the base in Honolulu. The number of casualties was still unknown but the number was already over 300. This was an act of war following the official declaration Japan made hours earlier.

"As of this minute," the commander paused to let the words settle in the air, "We are on alert. Our primary concern is security. There will be round the clock patrols and sentries. No one is allowed on or off base without clearance."

Though the sun was shining, no warmth made it through. There was a bone chilling anger and an undeniable need of retribution. The air vibrated with hostility and shock. All Vic needed was one opportunity of pay back. All he needed was a plane.

Acting in immediate response to the attack, all U.S. bases tightened security. In Visalia, cadets with ROTC experience in college were issued bolt action Springfield rifles and posted to guard duty. The next several days were spent re-learning the manual of arms and protocols. Flying had taken a back seat to imperative weapons training. It was expected that Japan would attempt landing on the west coast, in California, Oregon or Washington. If this were the case airfields and pilots would be among the first targets as planes were only useful in war if pilots could get to them.

The military tightened down on protocols and security and the rest of the country followed suit. Air Raid committees were established and drills were conducted. Newspaper articles on the war in Europe and now with Japan began taking up more and more headline space. The war was no longer a shadow cast threat over the nation, it was a full on engagement. People flocked to public meetings, military bases vibrated with renewed vigor, and people discussed the latest developments over coffee at neighborhood diners.

The new patrols at the training facilities were true military procedure and as such operated 24 hours a day. Vic and his fellows fell into the routine of rotating guard duty, flight training and ground school. The shifts rotated four hours on and four hours off. Sleep became a rationed commodity, reserved for those short stretches of time between guard duty and training. Security detail rolled through the ranks and everyone was expected to serve three nights per week.

Guard duty was the first disillusionment of war. The cadets had envisioned intense aerial fighting over foreign soil, sweaty foreheads, and laughing faces sharing a cold one after a successful mission. They had hoped to perhaps destroy an enemy stronghold or two and earn a few medals along the way. What no one had anticipated was winning a war by sleeping in wool flight suits on a cold barracks floor for a few uncomfortable hours before rising to begin another monotonous round of weapons training and guard duty shifts. The men were resentful and made jokes about their guarding being completely successful and not one Japanese soldier succeeded in penetrating the perimeter.

Murphy

In the wake of the attack, President Franklin Roosevelt and Britain's Prime Minister, Sir Winston Churchill, held the Arcadia conference in Washington D.C. They concluded to make the war in Europe first priority before turning the full attention of Allied forces to the Pacific. Thus, Japan met with little resistance and slowly advanced through the Philippines, taking the Solomon Islands, Singapore, and Rangoon. On April 9, 1942, outnumbered American troops surrendered to Japan forces in Bataan, and the Bataan Death march began. Of the 75,000 who began the 60-mile march, only 54,000 arrived at the destination.

War weary, still reeling from the attack on Pearl Harbor, and angered by news of the death march U.S. Navy pilots bombed Tokyo on April 18. Thirteen planes dropped four bombs a piece, canvasing the city. Actual damage was minimal but the psychological impact was greater. No fighters were shot down and U.S. military morale was up. These were the news stories Vic and his fellow cadets read as they prepared to join the war themselves.

By this time Vic had completed Primary Flight School at Visalia, and moved on to basic training at Merced, California. There, it was a completely military environment. Air Corps officers were the instructors for both flight and ground school, and Vic's teaching skills were, mercifully, no longer required so he was able to focus entirely on his training.

The basic training program at Merced was based on West Point and Annapolis. This meant that routines were ardently adhered to and enforced. Highest respect was paid to superiors. Honor and duty to service and country were at the core of the curriculum. There was a zero tolerance for breaking protocol. Even minor infringements were penalized.

The program was divided into two 6-week sessions in which the newly arrived cadets were the under class-men. After the first

6-week session of basic training they would become upper class-men. After completing the full twelve weeks of training the men then went on to Advance Flight School. As in any military academy, a certain caste system existed. The upper class-men could order the lower class-men to any number of indignities and they would be obligated, out of respect to rank, to comply.

On a random day Vic was striding in the late morning sun from one task on base to another, with nothing else on his mind but to make it to his destination on time and prepared. While his mind would have been occupied, he still would have acknowledged each of his superiors along the way with as much respect as their superior rank--a salute, "Good morning Sergeant," or curt nod of the head. On this particular morning upper class-man Howard Murphy was the superior who happened to cross paths with Vic. Without intending disrespect, or perhaps simply being pressed for time, Vic had slowed but did not fully stop in his acknowledgment of the upper class-man.

"Under class-man Tatelman!"

Vic's stride stopped short and his eyes squinted in distaste, but he did not turn around.

"Sir!"

Vic had no choice but to stop and risk delay in order that he be publicly reprimanded for his disrespect. His punishment was to stand at attention for fifteen minutes. He was instructed to stand exactly where he was and hold a salute without wavering. If he moved so much as an eyelash, the time would begin again.

Vic would have rather left the short upper class-man swallowing mud than to have been subject to this pointless order. But he knew that to defy the order would be insubordination, the cost of which would be much greater than fifteen minutes of senseless humiliation, and he would not risk black marks on his record. Vic held that salute for the full fifteen minutes. At the precise second he snapped his hand crisp and proper, shouting "Sir!" Without another word, grinding his teeth down in frustrated anger he went on to his intended destination.

Much later, in fact late in the war, Murphy showed up in Vic's squadron as a replacement, still a 2nd Lieutenant. Vic had by this time been appointed as flight leader and subsequently promoted to captain, as such he was now Murphy's superior. One mission, near the end of hostilities, Vic lead the squadron to Kyushu. At this point almost all the major targets on the island had already been destroyed. The area had been crippled and posed very little threat. The mission had simply been to find what few remaining targets there were and eliminate them. There were more blasted out bunkers and barren landscapes than actual enemy strongholds to be found. It was a rather uneventful mission--the kind that frustrated hot heads and triggered happy gunmen.

After completing the mission most of the aircraft in the formation still had a bomb or two left. The route back to base was over the Sea of Japan and at some distance ahead of the planes was a small boat with two people, an old man and his wife fishing for their dinner. There was by this time a major food shortage in the area as the shipping supply had been destroyed some time earlier. The local people had to rely on what they could catch or grow in the sparse fertile patches of land that were not destroyed by warfare. The boat held no threat, just an elderly couple trying to stave off hunger with a few fish.

On approach, Murphy was flying on Vic's right wing and radioed that he intended to break formation to bomb the little boat. Vic's immediate reply was an angry "Denied, hold your position." But to his complete disbelief, Howard broke formation, dropped low, and released a bomb.

Time slowed as it happened. Vic was helpless to do anything to protect the man and his wife. They must have heard the noisy planes above, and thought little of it at first. They were accustomed to fighter planes battling it out above their homes. They would have been focused on the water and the nets below their boat, praying for a good catch. When the sound above their heads changed the couple looked up to see one plane break away from the others. It wouldn't have been immediately clear that they were the target, but the plane kept coming closer and closer, straight at them.

In a dark moment of understanding the woman reached for her husband who took her in his arms and covered her head. There was no point in reaching for the oars. There was no way of rowing fast enough to get away from the thing that had just dropped from the belly of the plane. She cried silently into his chest. He watched as the bomb fell away and the plane climbed back into the sky, away from the expected impact.

By some chance of fate, the bomb went long and missed the boat. Sitting there in a small rowboat riding out the misaimed impact at sea, the couple wouldn't release each other for several long minutes. They were waiting to die, and would not be separated at the fateful moment. After the waves settled and the planes were no longer visible, they would have worked silently to pull in their fishing nets, empty of fish and torn. Neither would have spoken on the row back. The silent tears that squeezed out minute after minute would say enough for both of them.

When the flight group landed back on base, Vic was furious. The planes were arranged properly and the pilots about to leave when Vic ordered Howard to follow him. He wanted to choke the man on the runway, but protocol demanded better of him. They marched to the commanding officer's office and Vic debriefed the situation.

Vic and Murphy stood before the commanding officer. Murphy stood quietly at first while Vic relayed what had happened. He struggled with himself to keep from jabbing a finger in the man's face when recounting how he had ignored a direct order then bombed the elderly couple. The commanding officer, hands clasped and resting on the desk top as Vic spoke, took the information in. Howard Murphy, not a man to stand by silently when threatened, claimed to have not heard the order and denied responsibility. He acted as though he were the injured party, and insisted he would not have dropped the bomb if he had actually been ordered not to. He insisted that the radio had remained silent, as he broke away to eliminate the enemy target.

The commanding officer was wise enough to know a hot head when he encountered one, had Murphy arrested by the military police on the spot. He was subsequently court marshaled and returned to the states for a trial and sentencing. He knew that disobeying a direct order in a combat situation carries with it dire consequences. Vic was not about to let such a transgression go, particularly one so disgraceful as the bombing of a helpless elderly fisherman and his wife.

The arrogant upperclass-man who had made Vic's first six weeks at Merced so difficult had remained a tyrant and a bully. It was a trait that had cost him his guns, his wings, and a dishonorable discharge.

Precision and Advance Training

As Vic finished his stint as an underclassman and moved on to upperclassman status the war continued. After the bombing of Tokyo, additional American and Allied troops were sent to the Pacific to establish control of New Caledonia, Fiji, and Samoa. Army bases were established in New Guinea and New Briton in an effort to protect Rabaul. This was months-long battle that halted Japan's forward progress through the Pacific. The conflicts in the Pacific and Europe dominated the news. Headlines read thing like, *War Cabinet Ready For A Long War*: *Will Win At All Costs*, *INVASION!*, *U.S. Subs Score 2 Victories*, and *Churchill in U.S. And We Team Up*. Headlines were crafted to elicit emotional responses and took up huge swaths of the papers.

Not only were the papers inundated with updates on the war but campaign posters for war bonds and rationing reminders for everything from rubber to cotton were everywhere. One poster featured a pretty young mother and infant glowing like goodness itself. On each side of them, there were menacing shadowed claws bearing Japanese and Nazi symbols. Underneath the image, "KEEP THESE HANDS OFF! Buy the new Victory Bonds". Another poster featured a rugged and smiling soldier drinking a cup of coffee. Above him, "Do with less so they have enough', and below, "Rationing gives you your fair share." There were other posters too. Posters with menacing figures that threatened American lives, comical Japanese cartoons claiming happiness at learning American secrets, and many featuring children with messages about the need for their protection. American soldiers, women in factories, victory gardens, home canning, war bonds, defense against the threats of the axis. They were everywhere and it was un-American to not heed or respond to them.

Families all around the country were reminded every time they opened a newspaper, or went to the barber or hair dresser, even the grocery market had signs suggesting how to buy groceries in a way that supported the men fighting. Vic's family, along with thousands of others with sons training and fighting in the war, would have seen their son's face in every poster featuring an American soldier. Pride and fear intermingled in those moments before they made the decision to purchase more war bonds. Anything and everything to get those boys what they needed. Vic too, would have seen himself in those posters. But his reaction would be one of anticipation and hopefulness that he would not miss out on the action.

It was the spring of 1942 and he was nearing the end of his training at Visalia. He trained for precision flying with the Vultee BT-13. This was a bit larger than the Ryan PT-22 the cadets had used previously. The cockpit of the Vultee was encapsulated by a glass dome to protect the pilot and to offer a maximum range of view. The BT-13 was the most popular basic training plane in the military due to its speed, maneuverability, and 450 HP engines.

During the upperclass-men training basic flying techniques were expanded upon to include night and instrument flying. Exercises typically consisted of triangular courses, which were more difficult to execute than squared courses and were coupled with radio navigation to add another level of difficulty.

Night training exercises saw a plane full of sleep deprived trainees enduring long hours of flying in the pitch black of a moonless night. As the unseen ground raced away below them a voice scratched through the radio with instructions, coordinates and velocity requirements. This triggered a mental count-down to begin. After hundreds of miles in the air and a sleepless night they drew closer to the final turn and the last leg of immense course. As the plane approached the final turn of the course the crew rallied their senses out of the stupor that wanted to set in.

Vic's concentration was unwavering and his trained hands sensitive to the fibers of his gloves. He knew the grooves in his controls like he knew the ridged knuckles on the backs of both hands. He understood the maneuver must be perfect and never doubted it would be. He wouldn't accept anything less of himself. Minutes stretched out to impossible lengths as the coordinates were approached. The expanse of black in front and below the plane seemed to stretch out like the hallway to the principal's office in grade school. It seemed to take forever to get there, but when he did time sped back up again.

As the location for the final turn was reached the radio scratched again. Controls were adjusted and headings changed. The maneuver was completed. Vic's smirk was almost imperceptible and a bit lopsided. There was only another hundred miles before he could come in with another perfect landing.

After months in the pilot's seat, training, he was still waiting for the opportunity to serve his country, to protect his brothers, and serve up a little justice to the enemy. He read the news everyday and followed the advancement of US troops with envy. Would the war wait for him? He worried and ground down his frustration with more training, more studying, more routine flying. Soon enough he made it to Advanced Training at Stockton, California.

It was there the men honed their skills to deadly accuracy to achieve true precision flying. Success in precision flying ultimately means that the pilot is able to hold a steady and true course of navigation over long stretches to reach pinpoint coordinates. It was important to keep on target within time predictions and on limited fuel is crucial when flying over vast barren landscapes or open water. Given the eventuality of combat area take off and landings, both of which may be extremely short, the pilots were also trained on abbreviated runways. This is a critical skill to have mastered in that on many field bases or missions the pilots may be faced with landing in areas with limited or no actual runways.

It didn't matter how fatigued Vic may have been at any given time. He pulled himself out of bed each and every morning. No case of insomnia or bed head, regardless how closely it resembled a hedgehog, could prevent him from arriving fifteen minutes early to his ground school or advanced flight classes. His goal was to become the best possible pilot and he was not satisfied unless he achieved perfection every time.

At the end of a long week the men shared late evening beers as a weekly reward. A group of men in their off base uniforms would take over a table or two at some small bar or other drinking Schlitz beer from dark brown bottles, Golden Glow from under its blue and yellow label, or Imperial Beer with its signature parchment styled label and distinctive crown insignia. They tossed light hearted insults back and forth and wagered cigarettes over the next days' flight results. Vic laughed and poked fun along with the rest, but his thoughts were never far from the cockpit. His mind was continually reviewing training exercises, looking for weak spots and ways to improve his abilities. Though he enjoyed the banter, ultimately he wanted to be the absolute best and then push a little farther. He want to shine and then to own the sky.

During the last six weeks of advanced flight training, the cadets were split into two groups. Those who were to be fighter pilots continued with the AT-6 planes, while those destined to be bombardment or transport pilots switched to the AT-17, a twin engine trainer. The sounds of plane engines never ceased and there was always one squad or another being sent out on a training mission, or bringing back the results of another just completed. Vic's ears buzzed continually, even when sleeping, with the sound of those engines. So when the day of graduation finally came, the silence in the air was somber and somewhat ominous. It was a sign that the fun had ended and the work was about to begin.

When a pilot graduated from the U.S. Army Air Corps Pilot Training Program, it was tradition for the men to be pinned by a young lady of significance to the graduate. Most of the 28 men in Vic's graduating class had a girlfriend, sister, wife, or future-wife to do the pinning. Vic had only one real lady friend, a girl from Stockton. He would have been delighted for her to have been the one to pin him, but her mother would not allow it. She made it abundantly clear that it was inappropriate for her daughter to attend a graduation ceremony for a young man she barely knew.

What he did have was an uncle, a Naval Officer stationed in San Francisco. Not only did Vic's uncle come, but he brought a rather attractive young lady with him, a friend of the family. She was the daughter of the Palace Hotel owner in San Francisco. Her name was Barbara. She was sweet, and had a bright smile and playful brown eyes. Her soft curled hair was pinned up in the fashion of the day and the perfume she wore lingered in the air like a whispered secret.

In a long gathering hall with wooden floors covered over in neat rows of metal chairs sat a collection of women in colorful hats, uniformed men, and proud silver headed parents. Before the assembly the base commander stood at a microphone to deliver the commencement speech. High ranking officers sat behind him ramrod straight, proud in their uniforms and insignia, waiting to receive these new airmen into the fold. Vic and his classmates stood at attention in one long row to the side of the presentation stage. Their faces were proud, arranged to hide the joy and nervousness. They relied on the women, who stood in another group, to smile and beam each man's joy for him.

When it was his turn, Vic accepted the hand of his superior, offered his thanks for the orders, then stopped breathing for the brief moment when Barbara's soft hands reached out. She bit the corner of her lower lip as she fastened the pin to Vic's chest, worried she might prick him. She needn't have worried, he would not have felt if she had, elated as he was by her nearness and the gleam of light from his hard earned wings. The day was commemorated by a class photo in which all 28 graduates and their instructors stood in rank and wore their pilot's wings. Vic graduated from the Army Air Corps Flying School on June 23, 1942 as a 2nd Lieutenant.

The graduation party was hosted by Barbara at The Palace Hotel. The group made a sight all piled into three or four cars. The laughter and cheerfulness spilled from the windows as loud as brass as they pulled up. Barbara spoke with the kitchen staff to arrange a large private table set with linen, surrounded by dark walnut chairs and red cushions. The entire party was treated to a steak and champagne dinner. The servings were liberal and cooked to perfection, and the champagne was the best they had ever tasted. When viewed through the bubbles of a champagne glass even their drab somber graduation ceremony seemed like a fine affair.

Tipsy and still reveling, the men were offered over night rooms, so the party moved upstairs. The group moved from each room to the next, visiting, laughing, and depositing the room's tenants. Vic was finally left to himself, and he spent a few precious hours oblivious to the world. Rousing the next morning, he was still drunk on champagne and milestones. The party picked up again and moved to the nearby Marc Hopkins hotel to taper off late in the afternoon with more beer and glassy eyes.

First Assignments

June 4, 1942, was a turning point in the Pacific Theater due to the battle of Midway. Torpedoes, planes and dive bombers attacked and destroyed multiple Japanese warships. Allied troops continually gained ground and pushed further into the Pacific. On August 7, the first U.S. Amphibious landing of the Pacific War occurred in the Solomon Islands of Guadalcanal, Tulagi, and Florida, forcing the Japanese to abandon their bases. The elation of this accomplishment was short lived however when on August 9 the U.S. Navy suffered a major loss off the coast of Savo Island. Eight Japanese warships attacked by night and destroyed several U.S. Ships.

Further frustrating U.S. morale, on August 29, Japanese forces refused passage of Red Cross supply ship to a P.O.W.'s in Japanese held territories. The grass roots project that had begun in January of that year included bandages, millions of food packages, transfusion supplies, and medicines. Japan was more resistant to neutral humanitarian efforts than other territories holding prisoners. Only one tenth of the supplies that other territories allowed through ever made it to P.O.W. camps in Japanese held areas. Prisoners languished, starved, and fell to sickness in those P.O.W. camps.

Emboldened by these recent victories and an enhanced sense of pride perhaps, the Japanese launched their second direct attack on America. Pearl Harbor having been the first and subsequently the catalyst that motivated the nation to fully engage in the war, the second was executed on September 9. This would be Japan's first and only land strike on continental U.S. Soil. Two bombs were dropped over U.S. forests in Oregon. Rather than allow panic to infect the people, the U.S. government quickly censored the event from the news. The American people knew little to nothing about what had happened in Oregon.

Regardless of the nations seeming lack of response to this most recent attack, the Japanese government saw the bombing as a victory. The next major assault on Allied forces came on November 23 when Japan conducted an air raid on Darwin Australia. Japan was rabid for control of the entire Pacific and would stop at nothing to achieve it.

Allied forces in the area needed men, and the new graduates of Vic's class ached to have a chance at beating back the enemy.

Vic's first post after graduation was a disappointment. He was stationed at the Bombardier Training School at Williams Field (now Williams Gateway Airport) near Phoenix, Arizona. His primary responsibility was to fly bombardier cadets on accuracy training runs in the desert. He would fly in low over targets while the cadets sighted through their Norden bomb-sights which looked like the viewing and control sections of a high powered telescope minus the protruding scope end. Each sight was positioned in the glass bubble at the front of the plane, where the bombardier would be stationed during combat missions.

Vic flew countless runs, day after day, night after night, while the cadets sighted and logged successes or failures depending on their skill. The job was tedious and boring, the fields barren and remote. The plane he flew was the vaunted Twin Beech, AT-11. The planes were not built for comfort. They were frigid in the winter and oven hot in the summer. The engines were loud and could cause hearing damage. A person had to yell over them in order to make commands heard. The controls were designed for single pilot flying. So, with no co-pilot for relief a single pilot was responsible for every hours-long training mission. It was a small cramped plane and Vic, though glad to spend time in the sky, still dreamed of reaching the war that was still half a world away.

Precision was pivotal for the cadets' accuracy, and Vic's skill at precision flying, even when fatigued, equated art in the sky. He could maintain exact altitude, speed, and stability, painting a perfect line in the sky the way a skilled painter brought light into a still-life. The course would be plotted and controlled by the cadet bombardiers through the Pilot's Directional Indicator, or the PDI. The pilot was essentially following the directions of the cadet bombardier who would then be responsible for the accuracy of his own exercise. While the course was plotted out by the cadets, the stability and reliability of the flight was dependent on the pilot, and Vic's flying was always reliable.

Each run, day or night, saw the plane ready for combat and the bombardier cadet crouched and sweating in position. His nerves electrified nearly to the point of visibility: his teeth gritted, threatening to make contact sparks. Vic stared resolutely over the nose of the plane out into the vastness of the horizon. The bombsight was cold and heavy, and resisted adjustments. Sweat bled into the bombardiers' eyes and blurred his vision. He rechecked his settings, plot, and accuracy measurements. Time was too fast, the plane was too fast, everything was just too fast. Frustrated and jangled with thoughts of the looming war, the bombardier punched the information into the PDI. Vic read his course and adjusted the plane.

He was casual as he glanced down and serious as he adjusted his altitude and heading. A moment later, a single command climbed over the sound of the engine. Bomb bay doors opened and the enemy below was obliterated. After a successful deployment Vic banked to the left for a fly over confirmation. Both he and the cadet looked down on the blasted Arizona desert.

"Got the bastards!" Either one could have said it; and both smiled.

After weeks of isolation and routine in the desert at Williams Field, the mind becomes prone to wandering. Vic found himself day-dreaming about all the things he could be doing, and regretting his potential wasted. He was young, confident, and trained for war. Yet there he was, flying cadets on training assignments in the Arizona desert, no action, no freedom, and worst of all, no girls. The long "dry periods" seemed to stretch longer and longer. The days slid by in a slow litany of repetition and boredom. It began to seem, from the relatively calm interior of the United States where accuracy training was the most excitement one could hope for, that 2nd Lieutenant Victor Tatelman would not experience the combat flying he had so diligently and desperately trained for. He feared that the war would end before he'd see even a single day of combat and that his only service to his country would be flying in and out of training grounds.

After five months of waiting, following instructions and obsessing over the conflict he was not a part of, Vic was granted reassignment. He had spent weeks pleading, writing letters, and bargaining his way into a new placement. Operations had trouble finding enough pilots to keep the planes running for bombardier training and were reluctant to let go of what few pilots they had.

Eventually, though, his efforts were rewarded.

He was able to negotiate a transfer with the next class of graduating pilots. But no victory comes without setbacks. For the privilege of war deployment, he had to sacrifice six-months seniority and give up his pilot seat for that of co-pilot. Happy enough to be on his way to the action, Vic felt the sacrifice was small change, and he left Arizona for a combat group in Columbia, South Carolina on December 3, 1942.

Vic and two other pilots arrived in South Carolina a day early. As a treat they opted to splurge on private rooms in a local hotel. The beds were soft and made for them, the hot water didn't run out, and spam was not on the menu. Having just come from a base that was relaxed in their off-base protocol and not knowing the formal off-base uniform requirements of the Columbia Army Air Base, the men dressed down and showed up to dinner "out-of-uniform".

It could have been any restaurant in any city near an army base. The soft yellow light from over head chandeliers dimly illuminated the primary areas of the dining room. Couples or small parties were seated at tables covered with burgundy tablecloths and bright cotton napkins rested on the odd knee. Intimate conversations were conducted in voices low enough to blend into a background hum. The scent of culinary experimentation and spice wound around table legs or trailed waiters dressed in penguin uniformity.

Seated to one side of the room, at a private table with his wife, sat the Base Commander arrayed in his Class A uniform per the off duty dress code of Columbia, South Carolina. His wife, modest and lovely in her yellow dress and pearls, looked questioningly at her husband who had signaled the waiter. On an unassuming white card he wrote a time and location, along with a short order that the new arrivals he had spotted were to report in the morning for reprimand.

Three tired young officers were seated at a table across the room. They wore the Class B uniform per the off duty military dress code of Phoenix. They were smiling and discussing their new assignment when a waiter appeared with the note. Their meal ended more subdued than it had begun.

Vic's stay in South Carolina was, aside from the initial dressing down by the Base Commander on the first day, mercifully short and uneventful. From January to April Vic received multiple round sof vaccinations, and underwent full dental and medical exams. The men were tested in firing abilities, and weapons and equipment training. They were assigned to bombardments and flight echelons. Vic was assigned to the 499th bombardment and the 345 bomb group. He was promoted to 1st lieutenant and made the technical inspector of the group. As the group inspector he escorted the planes from South Carolina to Georgia and on to Florida for final inspections and clearance for war deployment along with the men.

The men were expected to report to Sacramento on May 1, 1943. They would remain there for a few weeks for the final preparation were made and schedules confirmed. From there they would leave for Australia, their first war post in the Pacific Theater. The flight from Savannah to Sacramento took 10 hours. When they arrived a full modification of the planes was required. Deicers and anti-ice boots were removed to lighten the planes for additional speed, as well as to allow for better altitude performance. Freeze protection was not going to be needed in the SWPA (South West Pacific Area).

After the anti-ice equipment was removed, the turrets and bomb bays were retrofitted to accommodate extra fuel cells in order that the planes be able to make longer distance flights. Long flights were common in the SWPA and fuel capacity was a serious issue. The trip from California to Hawaii would be pushing the limits of the planes even with the retrofits and extra fuel. Once they arrived to their war posts, the missions these pilots would most likely be given would include long stretches over open water or enemy held territory. Every ounce of fuel could be vital to completing a mission and making it back to base.

As the planes were being retrofitted information was cross checked and reviewed, including the flight plan. Each crew was given a manual covering the details of the trip. These included power settings for climb and cruise, mixture control settings for various altitudes, fuel tank changing and radio procedures. Two weeks were spent preparing the planes as well as the men for the trip from homeland to war zone.

The men were thrilled at the prospect of finally realizing their combat flight goals. There was a sense of urgency in the way they moved and worked together. Their hands were stained black by hours and hours of reaching into the crevices of the planes to make adjustments with the mechanics. Equipment checks were performed dozens of times and check-off lists were completed in triplicate. Orders were read and reread to the point of yellowing the paper.

This eager expectancy of deployment would have been recognizable to any other man on base. It was a unilateral human response to the anticipation of conflict, and the mixture of the elation and hesitancy that brings. This shared experience would serve as the starting point for life-long friendships and bonds. Too, it was a starting point for shared prejudices and cultural misunderstandings that would stand for generations.

As the day of take off approached, final adjustments were made in weight balancing, and plane and equipment checks. The flight crew assignments were reviewed and adjusted. One such crew adjustment saw Vic pulled from one plane and assigned to another. Originally he had been assigned to co-pilot with 2nd Lieutenant Cliff Bryant, a man he had trained with for only a few weeks in South Carolina. Rather than flying with Cliff's crew, Vic was reassigned as co-pilot for the Operations officer, Jim Banks, a man Vic would grow to respect and value greatly in the months to come.

On May 17, 1943 the bombardment group was ready for deployment. Due to scheduling hassles it was necessary for the group to divide and take off a day apart. Vic and Jim lead the first deployment and were to be followed one day later by the second half of the bombardment. They took off from California after exchanging well wishes of safe flights with friends and fellow fliers. It was uncertain when, where, or if they would meet again. But all were hopeful of sharing a beer and swapping stories in the coming months.

The weather was beautiful that day. The temperature reached into the low 70's and the skies were mostly clear. There was a storm that would come through on the third, but the bombardment would be well on their way to Australia by then. The Pacific Ocean twinkled below the formation that Jim Banks and Vic were leading. The sky was an optimistic blue that held the promise of adventure as they left the California shore line behind them and the vast expanse of open water yawned ahead.

The first leg of the trip was from Hamilton Field, in California, to Hickam Field on Oahu. The main stretch had to be done in the evening so that the 12-hour flight would bring them to Hawaii after dawn. During those early months after Pearl Harbor, no one knew if the Japanese navy had any carriers out there with Zeros ready to attack, so no aircraft was allowed to approach Hawaii at night. Night flying was particularly perilous as the lights of the plane would serve as a beacon to enemy boats haunting the darkened ocean below. These boats could remain blacked out and become virtually invisible.

Another reason it was provident to arrive during daylight was that wandering around in the dark over open water could be catastrophic for the planes and their crew. The islands themselves were blacked out at night, and as such there were no markers visible from the air to aid in landing. The planes had very little fuel to spare or waste looking for a place to land, and could not afford to waste it casting about in the dark. More than likely a plane would run out of fuel and would be forced to make a water landing. To go down in open water was dangerous enough during the day, but an emergency landing on water at night left little hope of survival.

The planes could barely handle it. Twelve hours of continuous flying, often against unexpected head winds or turbulence consumes a lot of fuel. No man aboard those planes forgot for a moment the limited quantity of precious liquid the plane was holding. The exhausting flight took a toll not only on the planes but also on the nerves of the flight crews. It was physically draining on both the pilot and the co-pilot as they had to remain vigilant the entire stretch in order to be prepared in case of an emergency.

Vic's nerves, and sleep deprived body were pushed to new limits of alertness and exhaustion as he scanned the seas below, read instruments, and plotted course corrections. He had flown across desserts and corn fields. He had flown across the country, and now across the Pacific, all in an effort to fly in combat. Had the flight taken even fifteen minutes longer the fuel supply would have run out and the plane he had struggled so ardently to earn a place on would have gone down before even making it. The landing was smooth, and the following night's sleep was the one of the deepest and most satisfying of his young life. He had made it; he was there. His life as a combat pilot had officially begun.

Days later, after he made it to Amberley field in Australia and then on to Reid River, Vic learned that the plane he was originally assigned to with 2nd Lieutenant Cliff Bryant had gone down somewhere in the Pacific. There had been no radio call, and no trace was left of the B-25 or the men it was carrying. The first of his friends to be taken by war had been swallowed whole before even making it to the staging ground.

Dirty Dora

During his time in South Carolina, Vic caught the attention of his superiors. He was a top notch pilot. He flew fast and hard, never missed the mark, and had glowing commendation letters. All this earned and more had earned him a promotion to 1st Lieutenant on March 26, 1943. He was given notification of his new standing and was set to fly his first missions with his new insignia. Almost immediately after, the wheels started turning for yet another promotion and he was promoted again.

After only a few months in the Theater, in August, Vic was again promoted; this time, to PIC (Pilot-in-Command). He had won back the seniority he had given up in order to attain a combat position. He was assigned a crew and given an airplane that had just been transferred to the Bomb Group. "His" airplane, a B-25C, was already named "Dirty Dora". Vic's co-pilot was William W. Graham III (Willie) and the two men were fast to become very good friends. The rest of his crew, Richard Rizzo, Gordon King, and Norman Walker, were all good men and they made for a cohesive tight knit group.

Dirty Dora would carry these men into combat and out of it again numerous times in the months to come. She was a good plane, and these men loved her. They were proud of her and told everyone they met about her. That was how Vic found out how she had gotten her name.

On one of Vic's leaves in Sydney, he happened to meet the previous pilot of "Dirty Dora." The two had been swapping stories and the name of the plane came up. The man was excited and more than happy to explain that the airplane was named after a girl he had met in Sydney, named Dora Bennington. Miss Bennington's profanity during orgasm he claimed to have been poetry. He had been so moved that he had named the plane in her honor. Some months later, by chance, Vic had the good fortune to meet Dora Bennington and invited her out to the airfield to show her namesake.

That afternoon with her well styled hair lit up in the sun, Dora walked alongside Vic. As they made their way down the row of parked airplanes, he pointed out this or that one with interesting art work and the Bats Outta Hell emblem that had been adopted by the squadron. Stopping in front of his plane Vic pointed to the name emblazoned on the side, Dirty Dora. She was perhaps expecting something else, maybe a hand painted representation of a girl on a swing with her name in lovely yellow script underneath. She was a little perplexed as to why the plane with the distinctive bat emblem splashed over the nose had the word, Dirty, attached to her name. She raised a delicate eyebrow as she turned to Vic and asked. Proud and pleased as punch to be able to have introduced the two Dora's he explained the name's inspiration.

Though the sun was shining and the sky was a shocking blue, a cloud passed over Dora's face. Her soft brown eyes hardened in anger and offense. Her secret was displayed across the side of a plane. She was a joke to the hundreds of men in the squadron. She would never be able to look at a uniformed man and not wonder if he knew her story. Furious at the thought of her legacy being flown across the Pacific like this, she turned on her heel and marched off in a puff of perfume and blunted dignity.

Biscuit, Bombs & Barges

During the summer of 1943 the war in the Pacific focused on securing New Guinea from the Japanese. In order to do this, General MacArthur employed a novel tactic. Instead of taking the Japanese through costly land battles, he by-passed major pockets of strongly held enemy territory by landing troops ahead of those areas. Troops were dropped by sea on the North coast of New Guinea, near Buna. Their mission: Drive the Japanese out of Salamaua and take Lae. This tactic was intended to leave the bypassed Japanese troops isolated in jungle encampments, cut off from supplies and reinforcements, thus rendering them ineffective.

Major Japanese supply lines were cut to be off from the logistic center at Rabaul through attacks by air and at sea. This included barge sweeps every morning along the coast to destroy what supply barges managed to get through the navy patrols during the previous night, effectively starving enemy troops into submission rather than engaging in costly direct combat.

In addition to starving the enemy out, Allied troops had to be provided for so that they would be in good physical condition. As the troops had been deposited ahead of the Japanese, they were in remote and difficult to reach areas. The landings that had gotten the troops there had been difficult to arrange and it was not feasible to establish regular resupply shipments by water. In order to keep the American and Australian troops fed and in good medical condition supply drops had to be conducted by air.

Supplying the ground troops by air drop was difficult as the surrounding areas were still enemy controlled and heavily patrolled. These missions, while not exactly combat missions, were critical in ensuring the Allied advancement through the region. The immediate Japanese forces did not have sophisticated anti-aircraft artillery, but they did have guns powerful enough to cause flak damage. One well placed shot had the potential to knock a plane from the sky.

These initial air drop missions for the Bomb Group contained supplies of food, water, ammunition and medical supplies. The rugged souls fighting for every foot hold in that disease infested tropical jungle depended on those drops. The medical supplies, in particular, were invaluable as there were more casualties from Malaria and Dengue Fever than from enemy engagement.

Vic flew dozens of missions dropping those life saving packages from the sky. They were giant gift boxes wrapped in dark canvas, suspended below parachutes that drifted down to Earth like the bundles dropped by mythical storks. Each promised to stave of hunger and disease for the grounds troops a little while longer, if they weren't decimated by enemy fire on the way down. The grateful ground troops knick-named the planes and their pilots "biscuit bombers".

While it was important to keep the U.S ground forces in constant supply of ammunition food and medical supplies it was equally important to cut off the supply line to enemy troops. In addition to continued biscuit bombing, Vic and his flight group fought from the air to prevent Japanese supply ships from reaching their intended destinations by sinking them while still offshore.

The men flew in formation, the planes to the front providing cover fire as those behind came in as low as possible and dropped bombs on massive Japanese supply barges which were equipped with anti-aircraft and strafing guns. Bright blue skies of summer days darkened with the smoke of oil fires and machine gun tracers. Ocean water leapt up around the bombs and bullets stitched patterns across the water surface in long strafing lines.

The plane that carried Vic and his crew rushed headlong towards their target. Vic weaved around anti-aircraft fire and machine guns that pointed upward at them. The route plotted and instructed by the bombardier was narrow and dangerous. Climbing up, dropping back down, bank right, bank left, hold on target and evade flak: All necessary within seconds. Still Vic flew on, throttle up and holding speed. Machine gun fire from below, and returned from the nose of his plane. Hold course, hold course! Bomb-bay doors opened, bomb released. Pull up, pull up! Smoke, machine gun fire, commands shouted over the radio. Vic pulled up and climbed. Enemy fire fell short. Bombs made impact. Ships sank. The men returned to base.

Biscuit bombing and regular barge sweeps were how Vic was first introduced to the war. He flew over large swaths of lush jungle, wide stretches of turquoise water, and rugged war encampments. He dodged machine gun fire and released his own, and his bombs alternated between life threatening or life giving. It was an invigorating kind of paradox he participated in, and one that would set the tone for the war for him. His time in the Pacific Theater would continue pendulum between bliss and danger, so much so that it would be impossible to disentangle the experience of one from the other.

The further North the war moved, more and more of their targets began to include Japanese troop convoys. Vic's bombardment had been successful in cutting off supply ships to the more Southern islands which were now in the control of American, British and Australian forces. Now flight echelons would routinely converge over hostile waters to prevent supplies and men from reaching enemy encampments, and leaving war weary Japanese troops in disease infested jungle swamps cut off and with little hope of relief.

The incoming echelons of the 345th bomb group darkened the sky with low flying fighter aircraft as they approached the target Japanese convoy ships. Just over the steady rumble of massive diesel engines of the leviathans, a slow building hum could be heard. The noise grew louder and the shapes in the sky more distinct. They brought with them another sound, that of machine gun fire.

The Japanese troops on the water volleyed their own return fire into the sky. But the U.S. and Australian Air Forces would dodge and weave around in aerobatic fashion making hard targets. Many planes escaped more than just close calls during these encounters, some suffered shrapnel damage and smoked their way back to base, while others suffered greater damage and went down. The sea devoured crippled planes with insatiable greediness. Those pilots still aloft fought on for their fallen brethren hoping the survivors would manage to climb aboard a life raft and make it to safety. Most did not. Those who managed to escape the sinking bodies of the heavy planes made easy targets for gunners of the convoy ships.

Vic did not stop cutting deadly paths until the enemy had been disabled or sunk. Every man in his group was similarly focused, each face reflecting the same single minded determination. Though their veins had been pumped full of adrenaline and their fingers were cold: Their focus, unwavering. They came in unrelenting waves from the sky, crashing down until the target was destroyed utterly, then flew away again as swift as they had come, reduced in number, but ultimately victorious.

Laundry Duty

At Reid River in Australia, where Vic and his flight echelon were first stationed, they had no ground crew and had to maintain the aircraft themselves. This meant routine maintenance, oil changes, fueling up, and complete systems checks. It also meant that if anything went wrong with the planes, they were the ones who had to fix them. It was not enough to just be a good pilot.

Before and after every flight, mission, or supply run in the planes, Vic and the other pilots of the group would climb into engine compartments, poke their heads into the landing gear, and check every instrument. Vic's dark hair, normally slicked back with a shine, clumped together and stuck out at odd angles by the time he had finished inspecting and working in the engine compartment. His face and hands were smudged and gritty. A metal tool box sat on the ground beside the ladder he stood on in order to lean deep into the engine of his plane. While working on and maintaining the planes, flight suits were traded out for dirty mechanics bibs with rags stuffed into back pockets. It was a time consuming job, and he was never more aware of just how much he had relied on skilled grounds crew.

Oil changes and refueling the planes were not the only additional responsibilities the men had to take on. A steadily litany of assigned chores dictated much of the daily life of the men between missions. Attention to the mess facilities, sanitation, garbage duty, laundry and grounds maintenance were divided between the men. Each man on base was expected to carry their weight and many times this included schlepping out the trash after noon mess, or delivering truckloads of dirty and laundered uniforms back and forth between the base and nearest town, Townsville. Vic was the appointed Laundry Officer.

To help with the deliveries, the RAAF (Royal Australian Air Force) loaned the base a few trucks and a jeep. They were right hand drive vehicles and driving on the wrong side of the road was something Vic struggled adjusting to. On hot sunny afternoons, Vic drove his laundry truck to and from the cleaners in Townsville. The truck moved oddly, turned too fast to the right and too slow to the left. He had to remind himself to stick the nose further out into the lane before turning left onto a street; otherwise he would have turned straight into oncoming traffic. He may have been an ace pilot, but driving on the wrong side of the car and street made him feel ungainly and awkward.

As Laundry Officer, Vic was expected to gather the laundry twice a week and drive it into the Townsville commercial laundry, of which the military had assumed operation. Each man's laundry was in his barracks bag and easily weighed 40 lbs each. Loading a truck with over fifty men's laundry twice a week, then unloading it again at a laundry had not been what Vic expected to be doing during a war, but the assignment wasn't all together unpleasant. The drives through the countryside were pleasant and peaceful, and on many of the trips he had company.

As a result of his laundry duty, Vic met an Australian girl named Daphne Fraiser. She was a WAF (Woman in the Air Force). Daphne was in charge of the military fuel station where he refueled the truck en route. In addition to seeing each other at the station they ran into each other during lunches at the Officer's Club. It wasn't long before they got friendly and Vic began offering her rides in his laundry truck into the surrounding country.

She was a lovely girl, with short chin length hair as was the fashion for WAFs. Her soft curls tucked neat and tidy under the blue small brimmed hat that was part of her uniform. Her uniform consisted of a light blue jacket with bright buttons and either a calf length skirt or pressed trousers. On her days off and during those forays into the countryside with Vic she more often wore a light dress with a floral pattern and exposed her light hair to the sunlight. Her lips were smooth and red lipstick made them stand out like succulent fruit. She was quick to smile and when she turned that smile on Vic he was heady with anticipation.

Those rides included a scuffed military truck, heavily dusted from country roads and military grounds, bouncing down a long and remote road between base and town. The windshield glinted in the sunlight and a man's elbow poked out the right side window from the driver's seat. To the left, her face hidden by the flash of sun on dusty glass, a glimpse of soft light brown hair winks out of the passenger side window.

With over an hour of open road between the fueling station and Townsville, seated side by side, the pair watched as quaint countryside passed by and got to know one another better. The trip should have taken an hour, but with so many lovely little spots only a few minutes detour away, it was so very tempting to turn a one hour trip into a two or three hour one.

The country, through which they were driving, was dotted with oasis-like hideaways. Vic and Daphne had a particular favorite. Only ten minutes from the main road, down a small dirt trail just wide enough for the truck was a small pond. The water glittered in the sunlight and the shore was ringed with eucalyptus. The warm afternoon breezes toyed with the leaves and cast shadows on the couple who lay entwined on an army blanket spread in the grass: Her skin soft and yielding, his hands strong and warm. They gave into their passion, pouring it out completely until they collapsed from fatigue, sated and sweating.

After a short dip, to clean up and refresh, they climbed back into the cab of the laundry truck. Smiling and shy, Daphne always sat a little bit closer when they left the pond. Vic, draped an arm around her slender shoulders and drove into Townsville happy to have her near as well as for the distraction from the war that had brought them together.

Shot Down

After Logui in June 1943, came new targets: Guadacanal, Salamaua, Kamiatum, and Alexishafen. The bases moved along with the advance from Port Moresby to Dobodura (near Buna) then to Nazdab which then became a major Air Force installation. These early missions saw downed planes, destroyed enemy bases and ships, smoking ruins and perforated planes.

In the span of 6 months Victor Tatelman was twice nominated for the Distinguished Flying Cross, awarded one of them, credited with downing multiple enemy aircraft, promoted to flight leader and captain, and completed 12 successful bombing missions. He had in a short amount of time built up a reputation as a reliable and highly successful bomber pilot.

On September 20, 1943 Vic was sent out on a mission to Bogad Jim, roughly 6 miles North of Dumpu and 40 miles South of Madang. The area was peppered with fox holes and Japanese machine gun bunkers that were slowing the U.S. and Australian progress toward taking Madan, which was on the North Coast of New Guinea. The job of the 345th, Vic concluded, was to eliminate as many of these bunkers and machine gun installations as possible. That morning Vic climbed into a borrowed plane. His own plane, Dirty Dora, was out of commission for repairs from an earlier mission.

As the formation reached its target they began pummeling the landscape and coastline. Dirt mounds protected the machine gun nests and made them easy to spot from the sky. Easy to see as they were, they were not so to approach. The little bunkers were capable of substantial firepower and the soldiers were able to direct it more accurately than Vic and his men were comfortable with.

The sky filled with bullets and shells. Bombs fell from the sky as the planes that released them flew intricate patterns to avoid the up aimed attack. Vic wove his plane through smudge lines of bullets that traced through the sky. One bunker after another tracked his movements with a line of deadly firepower. He flew in low, the bomb bays opened, and the bomb was away. Explosions shook the air and ground alike. Machine gun fire assailed the ears as well as the planes from all sides. Vic's attention was on the sky in front of him, avoiding another spray of fire from below. The air was thick with shells and bullets made maneuvering difficult.

The engine roared, his machine guns hammered out countless rounds, and headsets crackled with the voices of men in other parts of the sky. Everything was happening at once and all of it just as planned when a shell tore through the right wing of Vic's plane.

Metal screamed and engines shuddered. The sounds of a war machine dying choked out the sounds of the world around him. The shell had taken out the oil cooler and damaged the propeller so that it would no longer feather properly. Vic knew the plane could not hold the sky and grappled with the frustration of knowing he could do nothing to keep the plane aloft. Hostile water was below them lapping at the edge of an enemy coastline. He knew they were going in.

Vic aimed as close as he could to the shore and held the plane level. With both engines working, but only one propeller, he was able to keep his nose up and skim the surface of the waves some distance before making a splash. Graceful as a dancer that plane descended from the sky. She flirted with the ocean's surface, dipping one wing slightly then the other. Slowly, slowly, she crept closer. Wind whooshed outside, the propellers had stopped and the waves whipped by under the plane's belly. Then contact.

The graceful speed the men had known in the sky was interrupted when the plane tried to kiss the sea. The men slammed into their restraints, water rose up in great white foaming waves that broke over the windscreen. The nose of the plane gouged a track through the water that was immediately swallowed up again behind the plane. Air escaping from the plane boiled the water surrounding them. Inside, the floorboards were submerged; electronics fizzled, and streams of water hissed through sheet metal seams. Vic, his Co-Pilot, Willie Graham, and the engineer,

Norman Walker, struggled out of their harnesses and reached for the escape hatch of the ceiling. There were two men in the back, the radio man and the turret gunner, Richard Rizzo & Gordon King, who made their own way to the rear escape hatch.

Atop the floating plane the men looked toward the shore. It was quiet as was the sky. The fighting had stopped as each side had pulled back to lick their wounds. The men would have to swim for it and were grateful not to worry about dodging stray bullets. The beach was some distance away, but they decided it was not a terrible length to swim. Vic sucked in his breath and jumped in but stopped short of fully submerging. His feet hit a soft sandy bottom at only little more than waist deep. Incredulous of this stroke of luck he called out for the others to meet him at the wing tip. The men waded and chuckled to themselves somehow finding humor in being shot down and now having to wade in waist deep water.

They had not yet made it to the wing tip when Gordon whispered with urgency, "STOP! There are people there" and nodded toward the beach. He was right, people! They were too far away to make them out clearly and they were walking up the beach. The men stared out at those on the beach. How far had they glided? Were they still in Japanese territory? Were these friendly? How should they handle the situation? Vic stared for a long moment until he could make them out and recognized Australian uniforms. They had glided far enough to have left Japanese held territory and landed in the Australian's.

After a somewhat difficult and wet walk, they gained the beach. There, the head of the Australian unit invited Vic and his men back to base camp where they radioed the U.S. search and rescue team to send a Catalina flying rescue boat. An hour later Vic was on his way back to base and was working out how to explain to the pilot of the borrowed plane what had happened. The man never forgave Vic for letting the plane go down.

Photo Op

During the campaign for Rabaul while based at Port Moresby in October of '43, a mission was set for an attack on Wewak. At midnight Vic's sleep interrupted by an officer whose face he never fully registered. Vic received the assignment with little more than an expletive for being woken up and went back to bed. He was shaken awake again hours later for the briefing at 6am.

Vic and his group were assigned to take out the target's airstrip and destroy the base. The men were given weather reports, told to expect somewhat accurate anti-aircraft fire and a possibility of several Zekes. It would be Vic's job to take out the airstrip before many of the Zekes were able to take off.

An Australian intelligence officer laid out the facts for the men of what to expect on the ground around the target. With every mission there comes the risk of being shot down. That being the case there was always a designated extraction point assigned to every mission. The men were informed that if they were shot down they were to make their way to the extraction point and radio for rescue. The terrain surrounding the target base was lush with thick jungle that hid enemy bunkers. If a plane went down, it would be hard going on foot to make it the few miles to the coast where rescue could be expected.

With this in mind the Australian intelligence officer began his presentation with, "When you're shot down. OOOOO! OOOOOO! If you're shot down, make your way to this location."

The red faced man pointed out an extraction point on a map splayed out on the table before the men. Vic along the others assembled laughed, grateful for fleeting light heartedness the tongue slip had afforded. The moment was bright, but its light faded in the face of the deadly task before them. They had their information and filed out of the briefing tent to climb aboard the planes that would carry them into danger once more.

Six planes lined up, in formation, on the tarmac under a grey sky and prepared to take off. It had rained the night before and left great puddles of muddy slurry on the sides of the runway and between tents. The humidity was thick and hazy in the stillness. The trees hung heavy with moisture. The sodden ground gave way under the weight of military boots and jeep tires. The men went to their planes weighed down by the mugginess of the air.

Vic, as flight leader, was set as the first to take off. For this particular mission he was playing host to two photographers. The two men strapped in and hoped to get a few good shots of the bombing run. Vic and his crew were careful to clean up their language and follow protocol with extra attention. The Air Apaches, as the squadron was dubbed, had a reputation and the last thing Vic wanted was to make the squadron look bad.

Just as they were ready for the take off, he was notified by radio that the runway had changed. To change runway meant a slight reformation of the planes for the proper order of take off. This cost time. He was irked and his immediate response should have been, "Screw you. We're going to take off as we are." But ever attentive to protocol and aware of the photographers in the plane with him, he hesitated to send such a reply over the radio. Instead he adjusted his plane and instructed the planes following him to do the same.

He steered his plane around to one side of the tarmac, intending to drop below the waiting planes. His engines were running and sent vibrations through the ground, rippling the puddles that had gathered along the runway. Vic was focused on guiding his plane around the waiting planes and picking out the path onto the new runway. His gaze was elevated to see just far enough out that he missed a giant puddle right under Dirty Dora's nose.

Behind the second airplane his nose gear grabbed hold of the puddle and jerked the entire plane to an ungraceful stop. The men were jolted against their seat restraints and Vic swore through gritted teeth. He was still 90 degrees off from the runway he had been heading to. He was caught fast and couldn't get it out.

Banging the brakes didn't get work, pushing forward didn't work. He was stuck and nothing was pulling that nose gear free.

Frustrated, embarrassed and ready to beat the hell out of something, Vic gave it one more try. He cracked the throttle and banged once more on the brakes, hoping to bounce the front tire out of the mud and that's when it happened. The whole airplane went down. Wham! Right on its side! The propellers stopped short after cutting into the dirt and blew both engines. The nose gear broke off and the side of the plane crunched under the weight.

After a moment grappling with his anger and frustration Vic turned to his flight engineer, Norm, and told him to get the photographers onto the next plane. Then he radioed to tell that pilot to take the lead. Vic put his head down and ignored the sounds of bemused men's voices as they disentangled themselves from seat restraints and the debris that had been loosed in the tumble. The hatch was opened and the men ran over to the next airplane while Vic cried for the first time in his life out of shame. The rest of the flight group took off for the mission. Their engines faded to a hum in the sky while Vic stood next to his broken plane nose first in the mud. At least his crash had happened on base and he had been spared that several mile walk through the jungle to the extraction point.

Wewak

On October 16, 1943 Vic was again assigned a target at Wewak. The intention was for the planes to come in by surprise and take out the base while leaving no time for Japanese pilots to gain their planes. To minimize the Japanese response time the pilots of Vic's flight groups were to drop down low upon approach and skim as close to tree top level as possible. This would enable them to make the most of their surprise attack. Vic led the way, and brought Dirty Dora close enough to the trees to nearly trim the uppermost branches.

The base was cut into the jungle, a stark barren space carved out of the lush vegetation that surrounded it. Runways, planes, tents and a few buildings were what the men had anticipated seeing. What they found was as much a surprise to the men as their own approaching planes were to the Japanese. Lined up on along the tarmac was row upon row were new Yokosuka D4Y "Judy" dive bombers, Mitsubishi G4M "Betty" bombers, and Mitsubishi A6M "Zeke". The men had hit pay dirt. Destroying these planes would save untold numbers of American soldiers' lives, as well as cobble the Japanese air force in the area.

Vic set his target and lined up the sights of his .50 caliber machine gun. Lining the plane up for the most effective first pass, Vic set his finger on the trigger, keeping it light and ready. Willie Graham, who usually served as co-pilot, was this time acting as bomber and deployed the parafrag bombs that desiccated the grounds below. Willie released the bombs as Vic squeezed the trigger and set the guns spewing out fire from the nose of the plane. Below them the new and waiting war planes of the Japanese crumpled beneath the onslaught of the B-24s. Refueling tankers leaked fire and smoke billowed up from the destruction.

While the base had been cut into the jungle it was not far from the coast making it easier for supplies and reinforcements to reach the Japanese troops stationed there. It was near the coast and over the water that the reinforcements, who had been called in by the assaulted base, intercepted the bomb group.

Vic was flying on the left side of the formation as the planes headed for home when he saw them. Fifteen Zero's came in hard and firing. The radio burst into life at the first sign, machine guns spit bullets into the sky, and planes danced complicated patterns.

Dirty Dora's crew went into action. Their bodies sizzled like the very nerve endings of the plane itself. They were the muscle and in control of her appendages. Vic guided the wings. His voice was that of the engines and propellers. The Gunner twitched and swiveled the turret guns in the back. The bombardier and copilot serving as vital organs and spotting enemy approach.

There was no time. There was only sky and water and machine gun fire. The radio crackled and demanded attention that time would not allow. There were men in the sky and they were firing-- All firing. Ten o'clock! Ten o'clock! A Zero screamed toward the plane vomiting fire and bullets on approach. Vic banked to the right. Their bodies pulled against their seats. The turret gunner fired. Howe held the trigger letting loose steady streams of bullets into that air. They formed a dark shadowy arch through the sky. He traced the Zero for seconds before ripping through its engine setting it into a sputtering descent. The plane lost its grip on the sky and crashed into the water below after a long and wobbling glide.

The enemy disengaged and the formation flew on back to base with no American planes lost. Vic smirked as he pulled away: Another successful mission with no American casualties. The base at Wewak was caught completely off guard, so much so that even the Anti-aircraft artillery had been less effective than usual and the aerial reinforcements had been too late. The Japanese lost 82 planes, the air strip was unusable, the base was destroyed, and Vic would have one more commendation letter entered into his file.

Ropopo

The following day the men were briefed for an attack on the Japanese base at Ropopo set for October 18, 1943. Ropopo was on the North end of New Britain in Simpson Harbor. As the primary Japanese base in the SW Pacific Area it posed a significant threat to allied forces in the Pacific. Ropopo was heavily armed with heavy arms anti-aircraft fire, Zeros, and Tonies. Over 100 combat ready planes were kept on the base at all times. It was not expected to be an easy fight and the men knew that not all of them would be coming back. During the briefing the men's shoulders stiffened, jaws clenched, and breathing was just a little more difficult.

The plan for a bombardment of over 50 planes was outlined. The P38s were to engage the base first, hopefully taking out much of the ground fire and keeping the Japanese planes grounded. What few planes managed to get off the ground were to be engaged by the B-24's that followed and would plow an opening for the bombers to come in behind. With the path cleared for them, Vic and the other B-25 pilots would drop in, strafing the ground before them and dropping bombs as they went in order to pulverize the area. The primary goal was to destroy as many of the Japanese aircraft as possible, particularly the bombers. The men were informed to leave two particular airstrips undamaged. This would bog down the take off process of the Japanese making easier targets for the U.S. bombers. The tactic would hopefully give the US airmen the advantage of superior numbers and predictable targets.

The weather was forecast to be marginal at best, adding to the difficulty of the mission. The sun would not be smiling on them this day; instead winds and rain were to be expected. What they had not expected however, was a full on squall line reaching at least 12,000 ft, forty five minutes off the Dobodura coast. Vic and the rest of the flight group were caught up in blinding rain and high winds that forced the planes to skim the surface of the waters below. They were buffeted from all sides by giant fists of air that seemed determined to beat the metal bodies into new shapes. The fog that surrounded them that was so thick they could barely make out the indicator lights of the group's lead plane.

Vic's plane, Dirty Dora, skittered to the left and dropped without warning, making the men's stomachs jump up into their ribcages. Nearly losing sight of the flight leader, Julian Baird, for more than a moment was enough for them to question if the mission should have been called off. One B-24 went into the water. The storm was too intense for the rescue Catalina to locate the downed plane and seven men drowned. The B-24s broke ranks and returned to base, and the P-38s all aborted. The rest of the planes, the B-25s from the 345th, continued to fight through the weather. Of the 50 plus planes that began the flight, only 37 of them made it to the target. The bombardment, of B-25s that should have been preceded by a group of P-38s and B-24s, now flew in as the front line.

The wind roared over the sound of the engines. The water below boiled and churned, turning its depths into a foamed and murky void. Vic fought to keep the plane nose up and on course. He strained his eyes to make out the formation ahead of him and his ears for the crackle of the head set. His co-pilot, Willie Graham, hollered directions over the sound of the maelstrom and the bombardier in the nose shouted a single syllable response. The muscles in the men's backs were sore and their teeth clenched. Vic held firm to the controls and kept his focus on the limited space visible in front of his nose.

Unsure of how long they had yet to go before the storm broke, they kept on and hoped they would make it through without being lost to the storm. A voice called through the radio. The target had been spotted. Ropopo was just ahead and the flight was ordered to take formation.

As if a weather god had heard the radio call, the storm abated. The winds slackened and the blinding screen of water lifted to reveal the Japanese held island in the distance. As one the planes turned right and headed south to their target airstrip.

Fully aware that they were now more exposed than the mission had originally called for, the men screwed up their resolve and focused on the task at hand. The planes flew abreast, forming a straight line of deadly firepower, and primed their guns for attack. The formation swept down to treetop level unleashing hell on the unsuspecting enemy stronghold. Bombs exploded sending up mud, tree limbs, and battered pieces of destroyed anti-aircraft equipment.

The ack-ack that was supposed to have been eliminated by the B-24's, was intense but inaccurate. Tracer rounds perforated the smoke that rose up from the agonized base on the ground. Aside from minor shrapnel, Dirty Dora suffered no serious damage and held her course.

By flying close together and hemming themselves in, the flight group made one dangerous flight line as they rained fire and explosives down on the Japanese base. The enemy below was stunned, but only for a few moments. Crippled and reeling from the sudden attack, Japanese soldiers ran for shelter, or planes, or guns, anything that could protect them.

He flew so low to the ground that Vic's plane jarred and strained against the impacts of explosions below him. The reverb of machine gun fire from dozens of planes close in on either side shook the seams of Dirty Dora's wings and the seat that held Vic in place at the controls. Casings from his machine guns drifted through the air, seemingly in slow motion. He was aware--just for a moment that he would have to have the plane inspected for stress cracks when he returned to base. The thought flipped through his mind quick as the flick of an eyelash before he was brought back to the task at hand.

Below him was a landscape transforming from lush greenery, orderly buildings and tidy parked planes to fire, puddles of bloody mud, and crippled war machines. Great belches of thick black smoke obscured Vic's view and made navigating difficult. Below the smoke, slathered in mud, the Japanese base bled out, dying.

By the end of the attack all that was left were smoking

remnants of the Ropopo base. It had taken less than thirty minutes to reduce a key Japanese stronghold to a burning ruin.

Mission accomplished. Flight leader, Julian Baird, ordered the group around and back to base. The group turned in unison and headed back to the water, leaving the devastation behind them. As they approached the beach, a Japanese carrier came into view. It was an opportunity not to be missed and the flight group flew in hot off the Ropopo encounter, still armed and amped up. Coming in from every angle the B-25's strafed the boat. The Japanese responded defensively and 15 Zeke fighters grappled for the sky. Above the carrier the sky swarmed with fighter planes, Japanese and American. Bullets punctured metal. Air and water vessels alike struggled, but it was the American planes that were to emerge victorious.

Three of the Zekes were shot down and the ship was destroyed by machine gun fire. As the carrier bubbled its way to the bottom of the sea its massive form pulled untold numbers of Japanese lives down with it. The sea was dotted with men climbing out of dead planes and kicking against the pull of the sinking ship.

Mission reports state that the Japanese suffered the loss of barracks and supply buildings, 17 planes on the ground, four float planes, anti-aircraft installations, two freighters, and several harbor boats. Of the 50 to 60 Japanese fighter planes that engaged the 345th Bombardment, 26 were shot down. The tally for damages suffered by the US Air Force included the downing of two B-25s. Four others were marginally damaged but made it back to base.

The original mission for the taking of Ropopo had been organized and coordinated lead by Colonel True. Due to the weather, the mission had been officially canceled en route. Col. True who claimed three days later to not have received this information had continued on to the target. What resulted were a series of disconnected, chaotic, and seemingly random attacks on Japanese strongholds around the area. The incredible success of Vic's group at Rapopo was mirrored at other targets that day such as Tobera, an unmarked cargo ship in the Georges Channel, and Lakunai.

These unplanned attacks succeeded in crippling the enemy, but there were losses. Several U.S. planes were shot down across the area, men drowned and others lost pieces of themselves to the shrapnel and bullets that ripped through metal and bone. Vic and his crew made it back to base relatively unscathed, but they mourned the loss of their fellows. By the end of the day dozens of names were added to the growing list that would be honored by memorials and remembered by grieving families back home.

Prices Paid

With each target won and each move up through the Philippines, the war became less and less a romantic dream and more of a gritty and taxing reality. One by one friends failed to return from missions or would be shipped off to hospitals and replacements arrived from the States.

Through the smoke and fire and yelling voices on the radio, Vic saw and heard friends fall, trailing smoke like kite string. The rapid fire explosions of strafing leapt from the nose his plane. His bullets cut water and ate into the metal hull of ships or planes that had just shot down one of his own. Anger would come later, now there was only time for the mission, the bombs, the guns, and pulling his plane into position in spite of the flak damage that tried to pull the nose of his own plane down.

He sought exact revenge for each and every loss. For every American plane that fell from the skies Vic wanted to see six of the enemy gunned down. Vic and those he flew with saw this as their duty and right. As yet another US plane fell. They felt the cold anger of vengeance rise up in them. Though they may not have been able to exact every toll demanded for a downed US plane, they fought hard and let the loss of no pilot be in vain.

The battles continued and men on both sides were lost. Guns swiveled on the decks of convoys and bombs still fell on their marks. The water below boiled with dying planes. Massive ships pulled overboard men down into the depths as the sea belched out the stale air of ruptured below decks. Vic watched from the cockpit with grim unsatisfied anger as his brothers were swallowed in the same water that claimed the remains of his enemy.

The flights back to base were quiet, reverent of lost comrades. Smoke billowed up from the water or the decimated base then faded in the distance. This was the price, as far as Vic was concerned, for bringing down a US plane.

Shot

On November 15 on one particularly tough mission to Wewak-Boram, Vic and his squadron were to tenderize the surrounding area but were intercepted over water by enemy aircraft. The squadron, flying in route to their target, cut smoothly through the air. The even clean motion of the planes would have contrasted with the churning ocean below that gave motion and light to the invisible winds that whipped the waves into frenzy. Coordinates had been verified and radio communication was kept to a minimum. It was in this quiet calm that a voice from one of the men in the rear of the formation broke through the radio. Two Tony were approaching.

Vic's voice responded clear and curt. He ordered the formation to drop in low. The unmistakable Japanese planes flew in like white streaks from the air above. Trails of machine gun fire from the Japanese planes jumped up from the water below. The rounds went long, missed the entire formation to one side.

Vic and his men returned with fire of their own, up instead of down. They shot into the sky and watched as their own ammunition vanished into the blue above. Every plane, both American and Japanese, held course perfectly and not one turned to circle back for another shot. Vic and his men continued on to their target and the Japanese on to theirs. Two enemy squads on separate missions shared one point of tangency and for a fleeting moment machine gun fire was exchanged much in the same way nods of the head would be shared on the street.

When Vic and his squadron reached the target they found a small base cut into the jungle. It was protected on all sides with anti-aircraft guns. Vic had hoped to fly in unannounced and lay waste from above. This time however the enemy had word of their coming, perhaps a radio call from the Tony encountered in route. What mattered was not how they had received the information of

Vic's incoming attack but that they were ready.

Vic and his men flew in fast and began to drop low. Before he could make out the men running below, hurrying to their positions, Vic saw the anti-aircraft fire. There were flashes from the highest points of the perimeter followed by black stitches in the sky that moved in graceful arcs. The U.S. pilots wove themselves in complicated patterns in order to avoid being hit. They tried to get in close, to duck under the bullets and exploding charges launched at them.

Each plane was fully loaded with bombs and machine gun ammunition. The squadron fought with the cold intensity that only a seasoned pilot would know. They made the hits count and the bombs sent up plumes of debris and rubble. Pieces of the stronghold rained down on the Japanese along with strafing fire from the squadron planes. Vic and his men peppered the ground with machine gun fire, and drowned out the calls of the men below with their engines.

After dropping as many bombs as they could Vic gave the word to return to base. The men pulled high and into formation again. The smoking enemy base receded until the jungle swallowed it.

Back on base Vic found that his plane had sustained some flak damage. A hydraulic line was severed which knocked out the brakes. When he tried to stop after the landing roll it was like stepping on a broken clutch in a car ... nothing. The airplane veered off the runway to the right and barreled into the brush lining the strip. Fortunately for Vic, who could have hit a tree or run into a ditch, the emergency air brakes still functioned and he was able to bring the machine to a stop. None of the crew was injured and they all climbed out with triumphant victory calls. The close call served as little more than an amusement for the men.

Vic was a smoker during those days and it was his habit after a mission, when the engines had all been shut down, to pull his pack of cigarettes out of the lower leg pocket of his flight suit and light up. After climbing out of the brush and waiting for the plane to be pulled up and parked Vic reached into his pocket, as usual, for the cigarettes. He came up with a blood soaked pack and stared at it confused. He had been hit in the leg by a piece of shrapnel and felt absolutely nothing. He went reluctantly to the infirmary, insisting the wound was minor. Never the less, it was a week before he was allowed back in the cockpit.

Kavieng

One of the many targets in the northward progression through the South West Pacific was, Kavieng. This was an important Japanese base on the north end of New Ireland that served as the supply depot for the principal base at Rabaul, a refueling stop for aircraft, and a shipping post from Japan and Philippines. Most importantly, Kavieng was home for the submarine forces that helped supply Japanese bases in and around New Guinea.

Allied air power had grown significantly in the summer of 1943 and thanks to the thousands of airmen who, like Vic, participated in the attacks on Japanese barge traffic the enemy's supply dwindled. Due to daily barge sweeps over open water the barges were being destroyed faster than they could be built. This is why the submarine supply fleet at the heavily defended base at Kavieng had become so important to the Japanese military.

Vic's first mission to Kavieng, on February 15, 1944 was particularly rough. The strike plan was for the 499th Squadron along with the 500th to hit the enemy airdrome; then pummel the coastline to the North. They would then circle out to sea and pick off any Japanese shipping that may have been headed in with supplies or reinforcements.

The U.S. planes approached the base by flying in over Kavieng Bay. They flew in this way so as to keep out of reach of enemy ground fire. They were within reach of heavy anti-aircraft guns, however. This was expected. What was not was that the anti-aircraft guns had been modified so that they could now be tilted to fire almost horizontally. This made for greater accuracy on the part of the Japanese. The 500th Squadron, preceding Vic in the 499th, was met with devastating enemy anti-aircraft fire.

The planes flew in tight formation and crossed Kavieng Bay. The base was just within sight, but still just outside of their range of fire. The radio scratched orders to engage on arrival just as the first calamitous sounds of anti-aircraft fire ripped into the formation. The range of the heavy guns was a surprise, but the men remained in control. They wound their plane through the air, avoiding the incoming maelstrom of artillery.

Though the planes and pilots were seasoned and well equipped to handle any encounter, planes began to fall: First one; then two. The accuracy of the heavy guns was more than they had previously encountered. Tracers followed the planes through the sky at angles that had previously been impossible for anti-aircraft guns. The motions were almost liquid, agile.

Still they pressed on, flying in fast and hard. They dipped and swooped to avoid the incoming firepower. Another two planes went down over water. The sound of the radio verged on panic, "We're going down. We're going down. Where are they? Where are they?"

Crippled planes, 5 in all, splashed into the water. Men bled from the bodies of the planes into the water. They were exposed and now within reach of the Japanese. The 500th was in a bad situation. They were wounded and unable to rescue their fallen and were desperate for reinforcements.

The 499th were still on approach and about a mile out, but they could see what remained of the 500th, battling it out. In the water below Vic were the five planes that had been shot down by the Japanese anti-aircraft guns. Ahead of him was a broken squadron that speckled the sky and shot down at the ground in an attempt to take out the threat.

Vic's Squadron Commander called for the Air-Sea Rescue people and assigned a flight of three aircraft to circle the downed crews until the Rescue Catalina arrived to pluck the men from the sea. He then continued on with the remaining planes to the target. Vic was the Flight Leader assigned to the three planes left to protect the downed crews. The men struggled into dinghies. The dinghies were soon filled to capacity and several of the swimming men had to tread water until the rescue arrived. These had only their Mae-West to help them keep afloat. They were now at double risk of attack by either the Japanese or sharks. Keeping an eye on the men in the water, the Japanese shore guns, and approaching enemy watercraft, Vic had his hands full. It was only a few minutes before the Catalina radioed that they were on the way.

Several times, Japanese troops set out from shore in small motor boats trying to reach the men in the water. The boats rushed brazenly across the water, sending spray to either side and pointing guns upward in a vain attempt to ward off bullets from above. Vic's, as well as the two additional crews had little patience for the futile attempts of the Japanese boats. The pilots sprayed machine gun fire that punched into the water as a warning. Those few boats that did not heed the warning were punctured by the machine guns of the planes and had if they did not sink they were nearly swamped as they turned to retreat.

Vic couldn't imagine why they would attempt such a stupid maneuver, knowing the planes were above and strafing their shore gun crews. He had instead expected to see Japanese fighter planes at any moment. But the whole time they circled, none showed up. The Catalina rescue arrived within twenty minutes. Vic's flight maintained a tight circle, sometimes dangerously tight. They went on strafing with furious intensity to keep the shore guns silent as the rescue was conducted.

The Catalina pilot landed short of the first dinghy and completed his landing "roll" beside the men in the water. A hook ladder was positioned at the side bubble and brought within reach of the men who clambered inside. A fast taxi to the next group, perhaps 100 yards ahead, then a short take-off and landing to the third, and so on until all five crews, twenty-five men took-off. All the men were retrieved with zero fatalities. Seriously overloaded, the pilot of the Catalina, Navy Lieutenant Nathan Gordon, flew the rescued men back to Finchhaven safely. He was later awarded the Medal of Honor for the rescue of all five crews.

After the rescue Vic and his three plane flight group headed back to base at Nadzab. En route, they came upon a Japanese frigate that was most likely headed for the Rabaul naval base at Simpson Harbor. Vic radioed to the other airplanes to ready for attack. He led the way, flying in fast and opened the bomb bay doors to let skip a 250 pound bomb into the side of the ship. The other two airplanes followed suit. All three planes tore through the sky and the metal side of the frigate with machine gun fire. The bombs made impact, BOOM BOOM BOOM, and ripped apart the massive ship. The frigate, heavily damaged and burning, belched dark smoke into the sky and bled fire into the water. Crippled and dying the ship turned toward the nearby beach. Before the ship could reach the sand, men were jumping overboard and swimming toward the shore, escaping the smoking and red hot confines of the doomed ship.

While it was tempting to cover the churning water below with strafing and eliminate further enemy threat, the planes were running low on fuel. So Vic gave the order and the formation was forced, reluctantly, to head back to base and leave the enemy sailors swimming for land. Vic thought about what good strafing target those men would have made, but then he remembered the stories they had all heard of the Germans strafing allied troops in parachutes and decided that he couldn't be a part of doing the same.

The Nose Gun

In preparation for the campaign for the admiralties and the Battle of the Bismark in March of 1944, General Gunn (Pappy) had advised General Kenney, the general overseeing the 5th Air Force, that the B-25's and P40's would be better served to fly their missions at medium altitude. Until this point, Vic and the rest of the 345th had been flying low altitude missions at about 7,000-9,000 ft. This was very dangerous as the Japanese were quite accurate at this height. If the guns on the planes were swapped out with the Pappy Gun, a 6 gun, .50 mm forward pointed machine gun set mounted on the nose of the plane where the bombardier was usually stationed; the planes would be able to fly above the Japanese anti-aircraft guns reach. This would enable the US Air Force to move out of harms' way while increasing their accuracy.

In order to accommodate the new guns the planes had to be modified for accuracy and bomb sights had to be installed along with new bombardier stations. One by one the planes from the 345th were set aside for modifications and for those few weeks the pilots of the planes had to borrow planes from other pilots. For one mission to the Admiralties Vic and his crew had to borrow a medium altitude plane, bomb sight and bombardier.

Due to the nearness of Rabaul, a major Japanese stronghold in the area, it was expected that the flight would be intercepted on the way to the target. Previous encounters with Japanese fighters had taught Vic and his crew to anticipate being attacked from 11 o'clock high. This was the way the Japanese pilots were taught to engage and it served U.S. pilots well to be aware of the tactic.

Sure enough, on the way to the target, Willie the co-pilot pointed out that there were two Zekes fast approaching. There was no way to avoid them. The Japanese planes were flying along parallel with Vic at about 3,000 feet above them. The Zeke planes stood against the blue sky like dark birds of prey readying to swoop in for the kill.

Vic readied his gunner and told the crew to be ready for the attack from 11 o'clock. He alerted the rest of squadron by radio to close up. The planes squeezed in close together and as one dropped down low, as low as possible, to the water. The bellies of the planes had no guns to protect them and it would have been folly to leave the undersides vulnerable. As they flew the waves reached out to swallow their shadows.

The Zekes, having the advantage of altitude, flew past the group then swung around and prepared to drop in for their customary attacks. Watching as the Zekes moved into the anticipated position, Vic told his new bombardier to take position at the flexible gun in the front. He was to train his sights on the Japanese planes and follow them, but not fire until Vic gave him the order. The new man scrambled up to the gun. He grasped the handles with twitchy hands and swiveled the gun until the ring-sight encircled the approaching fighters. He trained the gun on the first plane and listened for his command.

In the cockpit Vic flew on and watched. The Zekes completed their turn and took position at 11 o'clock high. Time slowed in that way it does in a fight or a crash. All else fades into the background and nothing else matters but the moment. The sunlight glinted of the water below. The blue of the sky reflected back to itself creating one long and edgeless horizon. The Zekes gained definition and the sound of plane engines dulled from a roar to a hum. The moment stretched out like a rubber band before snapping back with an abruptness that continues to sting.

Vic could see the machine gun fire of the approaching enemy. The shots sparking like flint stones in the distance. Somehow the shots went wide and missed the entire flight group. Still Vic had his men hold. He was watching for the critical moment, that moment when the Zeke planes, being above them would have exposed their own vulnerable plane bellies. The moment came and Vic shouted through the radio, "Fire!"

He had given the command braced himself for the reverberation that came with the nose gun firing, but the reverb didn't come. The planes flew on toward the enemy and the enemy flew on toward the squadron. Machine gun fire went off around him. The water below absorbed most of the shots and the air stirred with the maneuvers as the planes passed each other. Yet somehow, inexplicably, Vic's guns stayed silent. He repeated the order to fire and still nothing.

The skirmish had only lasted a moment or two. Neither side took significant hits; and no men were lost. The mission was still a go. The Zekes flew right through the formation on route to Rabaul while Vic and his flight went on to the target base in the Admiralties.

The base was dispatched without much trouble. Flying at medium altitude as they were, the anti-aircraft fire from below proved to be futile. The bombardier sighted and set the targets below and the bombs were released. Dirt clouds struggled for the sky and men on the ground ran for cover. The buildings were destroyed and the air strips pulverized before the flight group ran out of bombs and headed back to base.

Upon arriving back at the base Vic, though typically known for his calm reserve, was livid with the borrowed bombardier. The men had barely disembarked from the plane when Vic barked for the man to explain himself.

"I gave you an order to fire! Why didn't you fire?"

The man stumbled and stuttered that he had been firing but the guns wouldn't work. He had tracked the Japanese planes just as he had been instructed, and pulled the trigger when Vic had said. But the damn thing wouldn't fire.

Incredulous, Vic had the man crawl back up into the nose where the two of them smashed themselves into a space normally reserved for one man. The smell of sour breath, metal, and machine blended together into the now so familiar scent that it went unnoticed.

Vic told the bombardier to walk him through what exactly he had done so that they could track down the problem. The young man slid into position and grasped the handles of the swivel gun turning it this way and that to show what his actions during the encounter. He held the controls firm and maneuvered the gun with a slight hesitancy that was partly due to Vic glowering over him and partly due to his inexperience. When he reached the point in his re-enactment, he attempted to fire by hitting the trigger switch.

The guns, installed in all the B-25's designated for medium altitude bomb runs, were Browning machine guns which had two trigger switches. Along the side of the gun, the breach was a switch marked safe and off. As the new bombardier squeezed the trigger he was also hitting the safety switch. So, rather than squeezing off several rounds of machine gun fire at the enemy, he had merely been squeezing the safety on and off at them.

It would have been funny if it had not been so dangerous. Not knowing how to properly use a Browning machine gun on the plane had left the entire crew defenseless against the attacking Zekes. It was a mistake that could have cost the crew their lives and Vic was not going to let such an infraction of inexperience happen again. He assigned the lieutenant to disassemble and reassemble a Browning machine gun over and over again for the rest of the day. There would be little danger of than young man not knowing how that particular gun worked in the future.

Olive

During their time in New Guinea, the squadron's leave policy for the combat crews was rotational. Of the twelve crews each had a week in Sydney every six weeks. The crew on leave flew its own airplane to Townsville, spent the night there, then went on to Amberly at Brisbane, and then Sydney where maintenance people were waiting. Each airplane was given a 100-hour inspection. Oil and hydraulic fluid was checked, the control cables tightened, tires changed if necessary, spark plugs were replaced, and all systems were inspected and tuned up. All in all it was a good thorough check out. Every six weeks both plane and men were given a reprieve and were refreshed.

With the plane set at the maintenance garage the men headed into Sydney. It was heaven to them: Hot water showers, clean clothes, steak and fresh eggs and best of all, girls. Getting living facilities in Sydney, for a week, was difficult. The place was constantly mobbed, hotels were always full, the restaurants packed, and transportation was suffice it to say, difficult. A young man in uniform could wander around town with his barracks bag slung over his shoulder, worn out and frustrated from hours of looking for an available room, swearing at taxis that rushed past, wishing he could just sit down someplace quiet and off the street.

After weeks of jungle rains, dirt in places unmentionable, and scores of fellow soldiers crammed in sleeping quarters on bases, the rush of a bustling town was disorienting. Cars of all colors zipped past hundreds of pedestrians who shoved or nodded their way down the streets. Through the doors of cafes, restaurants and bars wafted the scents of french fries, steaks, gravy and beer. It would have been a far cry from the smells of oil fumes and unwashed bodies crammed into sleeping barracks.

After months of bumbling around looking for lodging on

leaves, it was suggested the entire group find a house. It would be cheaper than hotels, always available, and more comfortable than leased rooms. All the combat officers of the 499th chipped in and bought a four-bedroom house in Rose Bay, a rather exclusive area of the city overlooking Sydney Harbor.

The city itself spilled along the rolling green hillsides. Hotels poked into the sky along the coast line. Long green lawns gave way to white sand beaches that stretched from one end of the harbor to the other. Long white boardwalks lead from parking lots and the roadsides down to the beach where families, children, young women and men sunned themselves and dotted the sand.

The house the men bought was in a neighborhood that was only a few minutes' walk from the beach. It had a low sloping roof, covered front porch and windows in every room. It was a gem of a place, a private palace for the men to relax and reclaim themselves; perhaps even take on a few conquests of their own.

They even hired on a permanent taxi driver, George, whom they supplied with gasoline, 100-octane aviation fuel actually drained from the planes. George knew where the best Aussie beer was sold, how to get drunken pilots back and forth, and where to find the most luscious ladies. He was a good old boy who lived it up with and for the men who kept him in good employ.

The first crew who stayed at the house lived it up royally. They not only found and bought the place, but installed three girls to keep the place tidied up and to provide comfort and solace to the "war weary" officers who came down each week. They saw to it the house stayed clean, linens were changed, food was stocked in the fridge and liquor was in the cabinet. The next crew, expecting the opposite, found the place neat, clean, and welcoming. If war is hell, Sydney was heaven.

A favorite hangout for American officers in those days was the Roosevelt Club, downtown Sydney. The bar tenders wore black suits, the glass chandeliers hung low and there was always great music. In later years big names like Frank Sinatra, Sammy Davis Jr. and Ella Fitzgerald would grace the stage. On the nights the American Soldiers visited there would be a large band playing.

Dancers took up a major portion of the floor. Along the walls were cushioned benches and tables where groups gathered for drinks and socializing.

It was there on one of his first leaves that Vic met a girl, Olive Wood. She was an usherette at a movie theater and they hit it off immediately. They danced, drank, and chatted with each other up in that way young people do. They spent the next day together, and the next, and the next. In fact, they got on so well that the two met during Vic's next several leaves. Their nights were spent mostly the same way, dinner, drinks with friends followed by long explorations of each other's bodies in bed back in Vic's room at the house.

During the days they walked among the parks of the city, or toured the museums and historic buildings. Once or twice she took him on a tour of her own favorite places including a restaurant with the best tuna steaks and a cafe with the best cup of coffee. She always had an interesting tour planned for the days. In the evenings they would stroll along the beach, or perhaps take a private table in a quiet restaurant. Sometimes they would share a bottle of wine with another couple and chat.

Their conversations never touched on the war, they were always mundane, the latest fashion, a recent movie, things of that sort. Vic particularly liked hearing stories of what it was like growing up in Australia. He also liked listening to Olive and her friends dreams of visiting America, especially Hollywood. Vic couldn't understand her every word, due to her heavy Aussie accent, but he enjoyed listening to her talk. She was vivacious and exciting. He felt energized whenever he was with her, he came alive. He was more alive with her, in a way, than he was even in the most intense conflict situations during the war.

An added bonus was that she was dynamite in bed. Fueled by mutual excitement and youth, their private encounters would last hours. She was demanding and aggressive; Vic liked that. With the lights dim, and the covers tossed, the two of them tangled around each other. She gasped and pulled him into her, savoring the moment and making it linger. He held onto her slender frame and breathed her in as they both peaked before dying down. The calm lasted but scant moments. Their bodies sweat glistened and their breathing still ragged as she reached down to begin again.

In the mornings, spent and exhausted Vic usually slept late while Olive made them breakfast of steak, eggs, and strong coffee with brandy. Those seven days of leave spent with her went by too quickly. In the long nights between leaves, Vic thought about his nights with Olive and felt his heart rate pick up and his skin warm in anticipation.

Unfortunately with the war moving north Australia got farther and farther away. Eventually taking their leaves there was just not practical and the men stopped going. Romances ended but the memories lifted the men up for months. The house too was abandoned, most likely repossessed for back taxes, but the men had little concern for such things. There was a war to fight, and houses were repossessed all the time.

Bob Post, Moory Victor Tatelman, Max Ferguson, Walt Burnes, Marty Wood, & Ed Egan.

Vic standing in front of Dirty Dora.

General Harris returning salute at Korean the surrender.

Vic with his graduating class.

The house built by a Philippino crew in New Guinea

Ie Shima through a B-25 windscreen.

Base at Biak.

Making repairs in Tachloban.

Destroyed Quezon Bridge.

Squadron area in New Guinea.

Air Apaches of the 499th.

Vic's graduation photo.

The 499th flying in formation. Vic is flight leader.

Japanese Convoy strafing target.

Clark Field in 1945.

Aftermath of bombing run in Manila.

Yalau

By March 1944 Vic had been promoted to Captain and flight leader. He had earned the respect of his peers and superiors, earned the Distinguished Flying Cross, been awarded several commendations and was nearing the end of his tour. It was policy that after 51 missions, active service men would return to the states with their tours of duty finished. Vic's 51st mission was set for March 5, 1944 the target, Yalau Plantation just south of Madang.

Yalau had the only beach in the area that was suitable for barge landings and so was of interest to the US forces. Unfortunately Yalau was overlooked by Dumun village, a Japanese controlled territory in the area. The village was inhabited by Japanese soldiers and served as a field base of sorts.

Vic and his flight group were briefed the day before that they would be providing cover for aquatic vessels and grounds troops who would secure the village and surrounding area. The men's job would be to lay down a smoke screen of white phosphorus on Dumun, then to provide airborne protection while the troops made their way to land.

The flight took off before dawn and in bad weather. They had to rely on instrument flying for an hour until they nearly arrived at the target. The flight had been so well navigated through the storm that the planes had arrived five minutes early. With this in mind, and being the newly appointed flight leader, Vic made the call to expand the mission. Vic came upon the village, still sleeping in the early dawn. The Japanese soldiers sleeping below woke when, out of a dream haze, there appeared the sound of engines. They were subtle at first but grew louder.

Without warning American planes filled the sky with the sound of machine gun fire and gunning engines. Japanese soldiers spilled out of huts and scrambled for the tunnels that hid the entrances to bunkers. Crazy attempts to reach anti-aircraft guns and airplanes were made, most in futility. Above the village Dirty Dora and the planes that followed her growled like angry beasts in the sky and continued to spit death down from their purchase.

Vic squeezed off round after round, eliminating the threat of enemy planes, anti-aircraft guns, and all attempts to knock his plane from the sky. The flight groups efforts were successful, the Japanese troops were so fully engaged in the onslaught of Vic and those he lead, that they had no notion of the water landing that was to follow. Making one final pass, Vic ordered the release of the phosphorus bombs.

White parachutes drifted down from the planes. From above, a long line of milk colored chutes stretched out over the airfield. If it had not been war, that sight may have been described as pretty until the chutes began to reach the ground. On impact each bomb let off voluminous clouds of black smoke that was thick enough to choke a person as well as blind them. The smoke was so think that from the middle of the air field the trees along the edge could not be seen. There would be no way of anticipating the forces that were making their way through the jungle with gas masks and heavy artillery.

Vic and his flight group had set fire to the village, reducing it to charred ruin. The number of enemy casualties was high, and those few that had survived fled into the jungle. Vic had completed this final mission so effectively that the grounds people had little trouble securing the village and the area. The stage was set for them to move inward with zero casualties or damages.

Upon return, Vic was nominated for and subsequently awarded the Distinguished Flying Cross for this particular mission. In the commendation it was written, "He very accurately placed his bombs on the village to totally obliterate any view by the enemy of the landing party at Yalau Plantation, two miles away. His bombs set fire to the village which was totally destroyed and ground forces later reported that enemy casualties were high: the remainder of the enemy force had fled the area."

Never Volunteer

Shortly after Yalau in the early morning with sunlight spilling unreasonably bright through the windows onto the grease stained concrete floor Vic was about to make a mistake. Mechanics shuffled from place to place preparing for their days work. The officer's quick strides were starched stiff by limbs trying to wake up. The coffee pot set at one end of the briefing area was surrounded by paper cups and bleary eyed men in uniform.

The operations officer had been up for longer than the rest, sleep grogginess rubbed from his mind hours ago. He came up behind the men and surveyed them before they even noticed he'd arrived. It's always easier to get volunteers when you catch them off guard. Someone was bound to hold a hand up, out of foggy confusion, and his job would be simpler. After taking a moment to take the sight in he started in on the early morning briefing with a paper in his hand.

"Anybody have any engineering training in college?"

Men holding coffee cups looked up at the operations officer. Some were semi alert thanks in no small part to the little bit of coffee they had managed to swallow moments before. Peppered in through the group were a few of the expressions the officer had been hoping for. An eyebrow or two flit up and down indicating sleepy minds working to understand the question. He knew not to do it, volunteer, but before he realized what he was doing, Vic raised his hand.

One, two three, four other hands lifted above quizzical faces. Outside the air stirred and palm leaves danced in laughter at the joke just played on the men. Sunlight alone had not been enough to wake these men to the realization that they had just volunteered against better judgment for a new and experimental post.

It was procedural that after 51 combat missions in the Southwest Pacific Area, flight crews were rotated back to the ZI

(Zone of Interior). The day Vic raised his hand in a caffeine deprived haze he had already flown his 51st mission and was contemplating what to do next. By volunteering, Vic's decision to stay on in the squadron was made for him and he was signed up for a second tour of duty.

Vic was ordered to report to Julian Baird's office a few weeks later. It was a sparse room that offered a shaded haven from the heat outside. Vic stood before the C.O.'s desk confident and calm. The two men knew and liked each other so there was no tension in the room or uneasiness at being called in. Even so, Vic respected Baird's authority and remained silent until he explained what the orders were.

Julian Baird stood as he looked over the papers. He thought for a moment then raised an eyebrow at Vic, who was standing at ease and staring resolutely out the window behind the desk.

"You're either in one helluva lot of hot water or somebody up top wants to talk face to face instead of communicating through channels. You're to report to the Pentagon in one week."

Vic felt a bolt of electricity jump up his spine. Something big was up if he was expected on the other side of the world in less than a week. In those days getting from New Guinea to the Pentagon was no small feat, especially in a week. It took days just to get from New Guinea to Hawaii. Then there was the trip to the mainland followed by another one across the country. Vic realized that his new orders must be important if he was to make such a trip just to be briefed.

Undaunted, Vic managed make arrangements and arrived at the Pentagon at the appointed time. After a year in New Guinea, which means no clean Class A uniform, he was somehow able to clean up enough to show up decently dressed. Along with George Mitchell, another volunteer and a member of the 501st Squadron, the two men walked into the briefing at the Pentagon for a new program and for their new assignments.

The men were briefed on the secret Air Force Wurtzberg Radar program. A highly specialized radar countermeasures program had been developed for use in the European theater. The Germans had developed an anti-aircraft gun linked to radar. The resultant fire power and accuracy proved devastating for incoming allied planes. Air Force missions all over Europe had to be halted until an effective countermeasure could be developed and implemented.

In 1941 the British Royal Air Force and Naval commandoes conducted a surprise raid on a German radar base that had been discovered through photographic reconnaissance. The ground soldiers had managed to secure pieces of the new Wurtzberg Early Warning Radar and captured a German technician. With this new information the British and American militaries were able to develop radar countermeasure that would detect German early radar equipment.

To nullify the accuracy of the German radar controlled anti-aircraft guns these radar stations were located using sophisticated radar detection equipment and then bombed to be rendered useless. The tactics were proving to be successful in Europe and were now being readied for use in the Pacific.

Following successful countermeasures in Europe, Washington began receiving information suggesting the Germans might have given the radar and the anti-aircraft set-up to the Japanese. Because of this it had become necessary for someone to be trained in countermeasure methods in the Pacific Theater. Vic was to be at the forefront of this initiative.

At the time the medium bombers (the B-25s and the A-24s) relied on tactics against the Japanese that were primarily low level tree top attacks where anti-aircraft fire, radar controlled or not, was fairly inaccurate. The enemy defense was primarily small arms ground fire that could sometimes be deadly. The heavy bombers who flew at medium altitude, eight to twelve thousand feet, only occasionally encountered anti-aircraft fire over the targets from larger caliber weaponry.

The concerns of the intelligence people over whether or not the Germans had given the Wurtzberg Radar to the Japanese needed addressing. If the Japanese had sophisticated radar equipment like this, it could prove deadly to U.S. airmen, and swing the tide of the Pacific conflict in favor of the Japanese. This is where Victor

Tatelman & George Mitchell would come in. They would remain a few months in the states in order to learn all there was to know about the most advanced countermeasures methods aimed at nullifying radar accuracy then go back to the theater and brief the combat crews on those techniques.

For four months Vic visited technical centers around the country. He attended lectures on early warning radar detection, different types of radar, ferret missions, and flying with the detection equipment. He traveled round the country again to watch crews train with anti-aircraft guns and learn about chaff release equipment which blinded radar. He even participated in test flights for radar detection from the sky. Vic spoke with engineers, designers, and specialists at the leading edge of the technology he was to bring back with him to the Pacific.

At the conclusion of their training he and George were given a little time before they were expected back in the Pacific. As a special treat they rented a cottage on the beach for a week. George had his wife and baby come down from their home in Idaho to spend the time together. Waves, sunshine, proper beds and home cooked meals where treasured indulgences that the men savored. The week passed in a quiet haze, at the end of which they decided to drive cross country from Florida to California, where the two men would ship out.

Vic and George bought a 1940 Chrysler for the trip and the military gave them plenty of gas rationing coupons. George, his wife and baby girl, Vic and a new lady friend he had met while at Wright-Patterson a month before, left from Dayton and set out for San Francisco by way of Idaho (to drop off George's family).

The little group took in all the tourist sites along the way. They stopped at silly little places that advertised the world's best cinnamon rolls or natural hot springs. They visited with friends in each state they passed through and leisurely made their way across the country. It was a small sweet taste of home before flying back to the land of war, plane engines, and deadly firepower.

Reaching San Francisco they sold the car. Vic and George reported for duty and left Hamilton Field in a new DC-4 on July 4,

1944 to begin their new radar countermeasures missions. Back in the Southwest Pacific, Vic was assigned to Section 22, the Intelligence Department of General MacArthur's Headquarter in Hollandia. The base in Hollandia was located on Dutch New Guinea, North of Wewak. There, he was given a map showing the location of various heavy bombardment squadrons, a jeep, and an A-24 plane. He was on his own getting to the squadrons and it was his sole responsibility to establish the early implementation of the countermeasures.

In September 1944, after less than a month into his assignment and still getting set up, it was determined that Vic would be most effective at 5th Air Force Headquarters instead of GHQ. He was transferred to General Whitehead's staff at ADVON, the 5th Air Force Advance Echelon. There his job was pretty routine, interview the pilots around the area and assess the accuracy of enemy fire, determine the level of risk, then write a report. ADVON, at that time, was on Morotai one of the northern most Halmahera Islands and the living was rough after the comparative comforts of GHQ. No hot water, outdoor toilets, unreliable canteen food, and lots of bugs. His second tour of duty, the one he had unwittingly volunteered for, was one of tedium, routine, and paperwork. He was far from the action and any girls, and he still had to endure the heat, and the dirt, and the bugs.

Life At ADVON

He wasn't long at ADVON, only a few weeks and still settling in, before the scuttlebutt (rumor) was rampant that big things were in the works. Sure enough, the allied landing at Leyte in the Philippines, though almost catastrophic, was accomplished. The landing was expected to be rather straight forward and decisive but there had been a critical lack of information that very nearly cost the U.S. troops the battle and lives.

When planning the landing those in charge did not realize a huge portion of the Japanese navy was holding only a few miles away from the intended landing site. Admiral Halsey, who was leading the Naval Campaign to take Leyte was in fact told that the Japanese forces were moving North, away from the landing site and didn't know that Japanese forces had actually remained to the South of the island. Having only half this information he split the U.S. fleet and took a faction to pursue the Northward bound enemy. The rest was ordered to continue on with the landing.

As they were approaching the shore no one expected to see a Japanese fleet come round the Southern end of the island. The ships left behind for the landing were mostly troopships with minimal firepower and little protection. Admiral Halsey had taken most of the defensive weaponry, planes, and warships with him to engage the enemy further north. If not for the meager air cover that was scrambled together, most of which were still in the distant Halmaharas islands, the landing would have lead to a catastrophic loss of U.S. troops.

Hearing about the fiasco almost-disaster as events unfolded, Vic and his cohorts, back at ADVON in the Halmaharas, could not understand the lack of intelligence. The men asked of themselves and each other, why hadn't we known the Japanese were coming around the South of the island? Why did Admiral Halsey drive north and leave the landing party practically unprotected? This was an example of the Navy fighting one war and the Army fighting another. Neither communicated the proper information to the other and troops were left vulnerable.

Vic sat grim faced at a table at the ADVON headquarters. His reports from the day before lay forgotten in a pile. Around him echoed the sounds of agitated men, curt orders and demands for updates. He felt the frustration of being unable to help vibrate his bones. All he could do was offer another set of hands to run documents, charts, field reports, anything to get the proper information where it needed to be.

Perhaps the damage could be contained, and the loss of life minimized. Hands were run through hair in frustration, grimaces were exchanged and gallons of coffee were consumed in those harried hours. In the Halmaharas, men were running with orders for planes, and men with messages from radio transmissions conveyed them hurriedly. Hundreds of miles away at ADVON in Morotai, Vic along with the rest waited to hear the outcome.

Against the belief of many, the landing was completed. The Japanese forces were beaten back. It was a U.S. Victory that almost wasn't that lead to a muddy beach off Tacloban on October 20, 1944. There General Douglas MacArthur waded ashore and made his famous declaration, "I have returned!" At the time one would have been hard pressed to find a soldier who would not have found inspiration in the General's proclamation. To a great many men he was, at that moment, God.

Following this victory MacArthur transferred his headquarters to the Philippines. It took only days to make this happen and in October of 1944, GHQ and ADVON were set up in the barely secure Tacloban. It was here that Vic began working in earnest on the Radar Countermeasures Missions he had been trained for earlier that year.

Japanese air-raids were an almost daily occurrence and the two navies were still battling it out in the waters around Leyte. Vic and the other men could hear the heavy guns from over the mountain ridge just to the west. It was disorienting to be surrounded by the mingled sounds of tropical birds, gentle oceans, warm breezes,

Naval War, war-plane engines, and distant heavy-gun fire. When the wind blew just right, caressing the cheeks of the service men and whispering to them in the voices of distant lovers, they could almost imagine they were in a paradise. Then the very next breeze blew in the scent of gun oil and engine exhaust.

ADVON Headquarters in Tacloban were housed in a conscripted bowling alley and was relatively comfortable compared to Morotai, where eating, sleeping, filing reports, issuing orders, and everything else was conducted outside or under tents. There was little escape from the ever present heat and humidity. There was no covering up that Morotai was a war encampment. In Tacloban however, there were roofs over head. Walls blocked out the worst of the sun's heat, prevented the wind from stealing papers, and muffled the worst of the noise when sleep was afforded.

The next months found Vic traipsing around New Guinea and Leyte talking to B-24 and B-25 crews. He learned from those interviews and from a few ride-along that the accuracy of Japanese heavy anti-aircraft artillery hadn't drastically improved. But it was less the accuracy of the fire that Vic was concerned and more the level of preparedness of the enemy that served to reveal if they had had an early detection system.

At the time, the Japanese technique of anti-aircraft fire was basically to send a mass of fire into the path of approaching bombers; then hope U.S. pilots would fly into the mess. Often it worked and many pilots were downed and lost. Every pilot at one time or another came home with shrapnel holes in his airplane. Every story of a pilot's close call was a vivid reminder of the shrapnel that had landed Vic in the hospital and of the many other close calls he'd had.

Hearing the stories and accounts of the pilots across the theater was not enough for Vic to determine the actual risk of advanced warning systems. He needed to see for himself what is was like on approach and how accurate the anti-aircraft fire pattern was. The pilots who were engaged in those missions were not looking for the details Vic needed. They had their own missions to accomplish and crews to bring back safely. In addition to needing specific information that only first hand observation would provide, Vic missed the thrill of real action. Although it was against the rules, Vic was considered too sensitive to risk being taken prisoner, he convinced a few operations officers into letting him go for ride along on missions. His level head would have been an asset to any crew he rode with. It was for this reason he earned the trust of the operations officers who granted permission for the ride alongs he flew.

The base was cut out of encroaching jungle. It was isolated and wind hissed through palm trees on quiet days. This day however, like so many others, was not a quiet one. The shouts of men's voices issuing orders and demanding a tight flight formation morphed into a dozen plane engines roaring to life ready for flight. The sun overhead was not a cheerful one, but an intense source of heat and blazing light that baked the ground underfoot. The backs of the men leaked sweat as they prepared to climb into the planes.

Vic was one of those men climbing into a B-24. He wore a flight suit and leather gloves and carried a note pad knowing full well he would have little time to make use of it. He would have to rely more on his memory for the observations he would use later in his report. He was assigned to serve as co-pilot on the mission and in this way not affect the performance of the plane with his otherwise added weight.

Twenty or thirty minutes after leaving base, flying above the green and brown patchwork of earth and field, the formation approached their target. The B-25's would drop in fast and low, spraying machine gun fire before them. The heavy bombers that were to follow had their own targets. Through the radio came a flurry of communication of how many enemy aircraft were in the air and the positions of where enemy ground fire was coming from. Hits were made and added to a cacophony of bombs, machine gun fire, and gunning engines.

Pulses sped up but hands remained steady on the controls of planes, and at bombardier and navigation stations. The plane dipped avoiding enemy fire and seeking out its target. The target was locked, bay doors were opened, and the bombs released below a spray of machine gun fire from the nose. The explosion was too far below to shake the plane, but the sound was enough to rattle the men's rib cages.

While thrilled to be amid the action again, Vic was careful to take in the accuracy of the fire from below and mentally mapped out the enemy encampment from above. He would analyze the information later to assess the level of serious anti-aircraft fire. He noted how much advanced notice the Japanese forces seemed to have by how prepared they were by the time the planes arrived. He took his notes and made sure to remember key pieces of information all while also acting as co-pilot.

He called out coordinates, verified hits, and scanned for anti-aircraft fire. He watched for flak damage firstly to alert the pilot and secondly to decide if it indicated potential risks of early detection radar. He responded to radio calls for cover fire and bombing aid, and reported on success or failure of explosions.

In short order the base below was reduced to rubble. Mission completed, enemy encampment dispatched and smoking, the squad turned for home. The flight back was quiet and gave
Vic the chance to scribble a few notes in his notebook, but mostly he just took the moment in. Back on base he returned to his desk to review his data and formulate a risk assessment. It had been a short lived but informative burst of excitement.

Aside from the occasional ride-along like this, and for the most part away from the action, Vic found life at higher headquarters boring. There was little that he could actually apply his new training to and felt his potential as both pilot and radar countermeasures officer wasted among the well groomed bureaucrats of war. There men stood among piles of paperwork making judgment calls based on mission reports and dispatch orders rather than by the amount of grit under fingernails or shrapnel wounds they had suffered.

He felt that the Majors, Generals and headquarters staff acted somehow superior to the men of the squadron level, perhaps even a bit arrogant. This left a sour taste in Vic's mouth and he yearned to return to his friends and old squadron. But he still had his orders and continued to make his rounds, conduct interviews, make assessments and steal the occasional ride along on the odd mission from time to time.

One bright spot during the time was that he was assigned a Douglas Dauntless for his tours around Theater. It was a sleek plane with one engine, a former Navy Dive Bomber pinched by the Air Force. It still had the dive flaps on the wings and that made it a bit distinctive among the twin engine Air Force planes that were designed for heavy artillery rather than sudden drops and combat acrobatics.

Vic took his assignment seriously. His face pinched into stern focus with his brows furrowed together whenever he reviewed the anti-aircraft information from each base. His calculations and research were meticulous. However after hours, even days, spent examining each particular set of results or squadron's mission reports and dealing with the red tape of HQ bureaucracy, those few hours of flying his Dauntless over land and open waters would have been a different world entirely.

Limbs stiff from repeated motions and military curtness felt lighter the moment he began his pre-flight checklist. Seated in the cockpit of his Douglas Dauntless, he felt a long familiar sensation of anticipation and his breath loosened to expand his chest wider than it had while grounded on base. The checklist completed and having received the all clear to take off he smirked with lopsided satisfaction. The engine would roar out in that way war planes did, reaching clean into the bones telling Vic he was about to break free. Gravity and land held him down no more. He was about to reach above it all.

Dirty Dora II

At the end of October in 1944 while pouring over data Vic realized that there was no consistent pattern of increased accuracy of anti-aircraft fire on the part of the Japanese around the Theater. He did, however, notice an increased pattern of early warning that suggested early detection radar capabilities, which could prove almost as dangerous.

Usually the first elements of the attacking formation found the anti-aircraft fire light or even absent in many cases. It was the later part of the formation that would typically take on the heavy AA fire. What was disconcerting for Vic and his superiors was that returning crews were increasingly reporting heavy AA defenses even before reaching the target. That meant the Japanese had in fact developed an effective Early Warning Radar.

He reported his findings to his superiors and presented a suggestion that would help in maintaining superior U.S. intelligence as well as military strength. His plan was to fly into enemy territory alone. Using the radar countermeasures training he had recently completed he would locate the Japanese radar installments and destroy them. By destroying what the enemy had for early warning systems, U.S. troops would be able to come in that much more stealthily. The risk to air crews would be reduced and the enemy would be handicapped. With his proposal he requested to design an airplane with radar homing gear in order destroy the radar stations rather than trying to thwart them electronically.

During his radar countermeasures training back in the States, Vic had been shown an experimental radar homing device being developed at Bell Labs in New Jersey. It was this particular device he felt would be most effective in the locating of radar stations. He suggested to his Captain, Mike Harris, to get the equipment, give him an airplane in which to install it, and turn him loose. The

Captain was impressed with Vic's idea and went to the Section Chief Officer with the proposal. In two days Vic had his orders and was clear to begin his work.

He was told he could have any airplane in the theater, carte blanche. He was also given the go ahead for any modifications he saw fit. Vic was then given the choice of which squadron he wanted to be attached to for rations, quarters and aircraft maintenance and on November 1, 1944, Vic was again attached to the 345th, The Air Apaches.

Since he had flown B-25's during his first tour of duty he naturally wanted one for his new project. Those arriving in the theater were the brand new "J" model. They had an eight gun nose and a pair of package .50 caliber machine guns mounted on each side of the fuselage making a total of 12 forward firing guns. While the fire power of the "J" model was impressive, it was the navigation table of the "D" model that was most attractive to and the deciding factor for Vic. The top turret of the "J" model had been moved forward into what had been the navigator's compartment in the "D" model. Vic needed that table for mounting the soon to arrive homing device. Despite the superior fire power of the "J" model, it was decided a "D" model was best suited for his project.

After tracking down the paper work for dozens of retired "D" models all over the theater Vic set out in search. All of the combat B-25s in the squadrons were by then "J" models, so it took quite a bit of poking around to locate the perfect plane.

Vic spent days climbing up onto the wings of one plane after another to examine the scars of fire fights, or poking his head into cockpits to determining the state of the instruments. Was the navigator's compartment intact? Were the instrument panels in good condition? He scurried in, up, and around dozens of abandoned, discarded, and left behind planes that sat in hot dusty fields. The old planes were parked in neat, orderly rows. These graveyards offered the bones of their sun bleached corpses up for inspection in hopes of resurrection.

For entire afternoons, Vic spent cooking in the sun, climbing in and out of dead planes, planning out different possibilities for his Radar Reconnaissance. After visiting several fields and inspecting more planes than he would have cared to, Vic was able to find a "D" model that was ready to be stripped and scrapped but was still in decent enough shape for him to reclaim.

He had the local Squadron Maintenance people make repairs and get the aircraft ready for flight. After only a few short days and two test flights Vic determined the airplane was ready for the flight back to Biak.

With the plane ready for flight it was time for him to begin modifications. Vic turned his attention to the radar reconnaissance equipment. He got in touch again with Mike Harris who sent specs to the Pentagon for approval. It didn't take much persuasion to get their support in the experiment. Within days the equipment and a technician to install it were airlifted to the Air Depot at Biak to meet with Vic.

The airplane was then given a re-work from nose to tail. This included an engine tune up and inspection. All the systems were inspected and, where necessary, repaired. The body was stripped down and repainted white. The work required was not extensive and the plane was made flyable in three days and brought to Biak for the radar equipment modifications.

The Shop Chief in Biak, in charge of the radar equipment install said the plane wouldn't be ready to begin missions for two weeks. The only logical move at that point was for Vic to order himself to Sydney for two weeks of R & R. He typed the orders himself and signed Chief of Staff General Southerland's name to it. With his forged orders and "co-pilot/crew chief" at hand he took off for Sydney.

From Biak they flew direct to Townsville, passing over the island of Papua New Guinea where lush tropical forests waved to Vic's plane as it sliced through the hot winds. The island's intense green hillsides undulated beneath him and resembled waves. Vic flew over the open water of the Pacific. The surface gave off a deceptive cheeriness that masked dozens of ships and planes that had been swallowed in the aftermath of violence.

He flew across the Torres Straits to Cape York and from there, down the coast of Queensland, was Townsville's Garbutt Field. It was there he spent the first night of leave set up on a cot in the bomb bay. His crew chief found another cot for himself in an obliging M.P. Office. The two men filled their heads with images of Sydney in an attempt to snuff out the images of war and the threats that new assignments would bring.

The next morning, while the crew chief saw to it that the airplane was refueled and pre-flight readied Vic borrowed a jeep and drove to the military fuel station he had frequented early in his first tour for an impromptu visit to an old friend. He was prepared to explain to her superior officer that a furlough was needed immediately for her. Vic's explanation would be he had news of her brother, who had just returned from the fighting in North Africa and was wounded. Vic was to escort her to her fictitious brother's side. He was thinking of the fun they would have during the time off, not of the fright it may have given her to hear of her brother's false injury.

When Vic arrived, all officiousness and salutes, he was informed she was no longer there. Nobody knew where she had been sent. There he was, standing before some vaguely curious official in a Royal Australian Air Force (RAAF) uniform. Vic's expression stoic and firm with his eyebrows carefully impassive while he explained he was looking for a particular young lady and that he carried news to be delivered directly to her. The RAAF man, confused at the lack of information this young American officer had pertaining to his assignment, listened patiently before informing him of the girl's transfer. Vic was frustrated and felt a little silly for having driven an hour in the muggy heat of Northern Australia looking for a girl that was no longer there. He excused himself and returned to his truck. It was probably just as well she wasn't there as he wasn't prepared to explain what his part, an American soldier with official news of an Australian soldier's injury, in all this was.

In spite of not being able to find his friend, Vic spent a marvelous two weeks in Sydney. He ran into old friends and spent evenings eating and drinking with new friends in old familiar places. The girls were sweet and lovely, so much so that he soon forgot the girl in Townsville. But like all leaves that came before, this one too had to end. He left Sydney that paradise city, with clean sheets, fine hotels, hot water showers, steak and egg breakfasts, liquor and girls, reluctantly.

Back in Biak Vic went to retrieve his plane. He along, with the head mechanic, moved through the depot with purpose. It was a long metal building with shadowed corners dark enough to distort faces. Through this shaded military reserve of war planes, engines, and broken parts, Vic's footsteps echoed and faded out on the far end. The two men's voices stirred the dust as they moved through the discarded instruments of war.

The plane modifications he had requested were complete and his plane was ready to for the radar equipment. The glass bombardier's nose of his "D" model plane had been replaced by an eight gun "J" Model nose; and the inverter switch moved from the bomb bay bulkhead to the lower left instrument panel so that Vic could reach it without leaving the cockpit. He had also requested that a turret tank be installed that would allow for two extra hours of fuel. There was a jump seat installed for the radar operator, and most importantly, the radar equipment was installed on the old navigator's table. With the modifications complete, everything was ready for testing.

Fortunately for Vic and his project, not only did Bell Labs send the equipment, but also a technician, Dick Wolfe, who was eager for the test flights. He was a young man, about the same age as Vic, with dark hair and a firm expression. His full lips that smiled so easily back home were slow to do so here when so much was at stake. The two men made a good team, the pilot gazing grimly down on the jungle landscape searching for visual clues of the enemy's radar stations, and the tech with a similar expression reading coordinates and homing device results. Information would be passed in single syllables and nods of the head--a form of communication that only the initiates of combat flying have been able to achieve.

They flew several local flights testing for accuracy against the military's own radars in the area. The equipment was adjusted, tested, flown, tested and adjusted again. The entire project depended on this phase and the accuracy of the radar equipment; otherwise, the entire project would be pointless.

The day after another set of adjustments had been made, Vic scheduled a test run. The sun blazed above attempting to burn an opening in the canopy of the jungles below, but the trees resisted, angry at the attempt to be pierced. Vic's eyes couldn't make out precise locations of the anti-aircraft radar below. The equipment mounted in front of Wolfe however, did not fight the same battle. It could reach straight down to the earth below, piercing through canopy and inclement weather to tell the men precisely where to fly in low.

Vic dropped in altitude, passed over the designated area, photographed the site and executed a mock fire to destroy the station. He banked to the left and returned to base. Both men smiled knowing that the final adjustments had been successful and everything was ready for combat.

Testing done, Wolfe spoke to somebody with authority into letting him stay in the theater. It was his intention to fly with Vic, operate and maintain the equipment once combat operations began. In spite of being a civilian, he was authorized to remain in the Pacific for the countermeasures missions. Vic felt this a fortunate turn as Wolfe was a genius with the equipment.

Vic had already made arrangements to be returned to his old Squadron, the 499th Bomb Squadron of the 345th Bomb group, AKA The Air Apaches, which was by then based at San Marceline in Luzon, so he and Wolfe set out for their new base. Vic flew his new B-25 to San Marcelino expecting to see all his old friends, but alas, they were mostly gone. Combat crews were rotated back to the States after 51 missions and a whole new generation of combat crews now made up the Squadron. He was back with his old squadron, but he was among strangers almost as completely as he had been at HQ. It hadn't even crossed his mind that the old combat crews had completed their required 51 missions and returned to the states.

It was a little disorienting to have expected to come across faces that lit up with recognition and friendly smiles. Instead he again and again saw only blank expressions on strangers' faces. He walked through the encampment of airmen, hearing men volley back and forth friendly taunts but was unable to join in as he had in the past. Hot muggy air was pressing down on everyone making their faces gleam with sweat and blending them into one long stream of unrecognizable faces--just one more dirty war encampment full of war weary men and battered gear: Familiar in its unfamiliarity but little more.

Upon arrival Vic was expected to report to the new Commander, Wendell Decker. In the man's tent Vic found three men clustered around a table studying maps and mission reports. One was talking in a low tone and pointing out locations of importance on the map, the other two men nodded with brows creased and offered their input. Their speech was indiscernible from the distance, the mix of deep voices rumbled through the air giving the tent a serious atmosphere.

One of them looked up as Vic approached, the line between his eyebrows unfolding in surprise. He elbowed the man to his left who, after looking up, threw his head back in a bark of amusement. Vic smiled and extended his hand, which each of the three men grasped in welcome.

Marty Wood was still the Executive Officer, he and the other ground officers (Section Heads: Engineering, Communications, Armament and so forth) were still carrying on. Since they were all who was left of the original Squadron, Vic moved into their tent, glad to be among friends. He later found a few more familiar faces with the mechanics and was assigned his old ground crew who promptly named his airplane Dirty Dora II. They even painted the squadron's distinctive bat emblem on the nose.

The General's Plane

After relocating to San Marceline, while waiting to HQ to get set up and send his first FRAG orders, the operations people at ADVON put out a call for a pilot who was checked-out in C-45 aircraft, which Vic was. He had over 1,000 hours in AT-lls--a similar aircraft, from his time flying with the bombardier trainees over the deserts back in the states. This made him more than qualified and it offered to break up the time he had to spend waiting for his first frag-orders to come through an office not yet set up, so he volunteered to go.

General Whitehead's personal airplane had been brought over, disassembled, from the States to the Air Depot at Biak for reassembly and testing. It was being fitted out for executive transport which included quite a few luxuries at the cost of fuel capacity and gunning capabilities. By the time Vic volunteered for the task, the plane was ready and waiting. All he was expected to do, according to the officials, was show up, and fly it out.

Vic left his "new" B-25 where it was waiting to be deployed and hopped a C-47 back to Biak. He looked up a test pilot friend, Jack Riley, who had just test flown the very C-45 Vic was there to transport and pronounced it fit to go. However, there was a big problem that had gone unnoticed until Vic arrived to point it out. The modifications and added luxuries meant that the plane couldn't carry enough fuel to make the trip to General Whitehead's offices in the Philippines.

In order to get the plane to the destination from Biak, Vic would need an extra 35 gallon fuel tank installed. He suggested mounting a fighter belly tank in the cabin, where there had just been installed a lovely set of plush cabin seats. They were the kind that makes a person sigh when sitting down, the kind that bomber pilots never see. The mechanics took out all those plush cabin seats with amusement and a little envy, built a cradle on the cabin floor, and mounted a P-40 drop tank in their place.

A fuel line and pump were then installed in order to transfer the fuel through the cabin wall and into the right wing fuel tank. The pump switch was located within reach of the pilot seat so that Vic wouldn't have to leave the cockpit. The 35 gallons should be more than enough to make the trip possible, but Vic was leaving nothing to chance. As a safety precaution he fitted the cabin, near the door, with a 5-man life raft and a 5-gallon Jerry can of water, just in case. There's a lot of ocean between Biak and the Philippines and the last thing he wanted was to run out of fuel over open water without some sort of life raft and drinking water.

Modifications finished and fail safes in place, Vic climbed into the cockpit. He ran the usual preflight checklist, crossed his fingers that the extra fuel was not only enough but would transfer properly once he flipped the switch, and took off. The engines growled into life, grew in pitch, and vibrated his bones. The sky was bright and enticing above him. Smiling, Vic gunned it. Racing down the runway he challenged the open skies to a race then lifted off the ground smooth and swift. He was in his element. The feeling after take-off was the same every time, peace.

After reaching altitude Vic noticed a C-47 just ahead flying the same course. He flew up on the wing and radioed to inquire their destination. Finding that they were heading to the same place Vic requested and was permitted to fly alongside the C-47 and was relieved of having to navigate himself.

En route he burned the fuel in the right main tank and flipped the switch for the fuel transfer to refill the tank but the transfer did not happen. His fuel kept draining from the already dwindling fuel tank and the reserves were left untouched. Realizing this he called the C-47 and the navigator aboard gave Vic a heading to the nearest airfield; Sansapor on the extreme northwest tip of New Guinea. With enough barely fuel in the left tank to cover the distance, he broke off.

Seated in the sky with nothing but a vast expanse of saltwater hundreds of feet below, a dropping fuel level, and an un-accessible reserve tank right behind the seat would have been enough to panic many men. Fear would quicken any man's breath as he listened for the inevitable sound of a choking engine, ready and braced for the plane to lose its grasp of the sky. Vic was not such a man and the situation was more irksome than frightening. He kept his head and conceded a point to chance, but chance would not win the game. Vic was too well prepared, too well trained, and too composed to lose control.

He made it to a base in Sansapor with little fuel to spare and had the problem looked into. It was discovered on inspection that someone at the Biak depot had inadvertently used a rubber gasket that was not compatible with the fuel. It had swelled up, choking off the fuel flow and was a relatively easy fix that caused only a slight delay.

After Sansapor he flew on to Tacloban and was told there to take the airplane on to Mindoro. It was at Mindoro that General Whitehead planned to move his headquarters, anticipating an early move to Manila. Aside from the surprise detour spurred by a rubber gasket, Vic got the airplane to its destination, minus the plush seats.

First Radar Countermeasures

While based at San Marcelino, Vic began receiving the first of his Frag Orders from 5th Air Force Intelligence for his radar countermeasures missions. A crew of volunteers was selected from the Squadron; Byron Reed as co-pilot, Richard Gemmill as navigator, Arthur Schaffer as radar operations, John White as Engineer, and Palmer Anthony as radio operations. Along with Dick Wolfe, the radar homing equipment operator who had been sent from the States, they set off on the first of what were to be called "ferret" missions.

When the first frag-orders came in, they scoured the area, but came up with nothing. Undaunted by the lack of results they set out again when the second set of orders came in. Again, nothing but bristling jungles below, abandoned enemy encampments, and scattered villages. By the third order, however, the men hit pay dirt.

An early warning radar was suspected on Babuyan, just north of Luzon. Vic and his crew hoped to find something substantial but were unable to let go of the doubts the previous two missions had embedded and they doubted anything would come of this mission either.

The engines roared on either side of the cockpit. The co-pilot, Byron Reed, scanned the skies and ground below for enemy fire. The radar homing equipment was showing signs of life and traced their progress in blips. The trees below knit unto themselves, trying to keep its secrets from prying eyes. Unable to hide from the homing device though, the jungle gave up its secret and parted the canopy.

The Homing equipment brought them closer and closer to a pinpoint location. It was Reed who pointed out what they had been looking for. It was a rude field base with a small building that served as the radar station. It was protected by ground fire, earthen barricades, and enemy secrecy. None of which were able to shield it from the firepower the plane carried.

Vic swooped in fast and low, avoiding enemy fire and took pictures with the K-21 automatic camera that had been mounted near the tail of the airplane. He pulled up and gave the order to prepare for fire, then came in again to disable the radar. Men on the ground scrambled. There was a helter-skelter of defensive fire, but nothing to prove very dangerous to Vic or his crew. In less than five minutes the installation was discovered, photographed, and destroyed.

Encouraged by their first successful mission Vic headed back to base. All his time spent flying around the Pacific interviewing theater pilots, compiling reports, and proposing his idea on how to handle the Japanese radar threat had gone into making this project possible. He had in a single mission achieved more for the U.S. forces than he had in two dozen interviews.

Prior to receiving any frag orders, Vic had been instructed by General Hogan to thoroughly photograph any sites prior to destroying them. The intelligence people desperately wanted the photographs to determine types of radar, the shape and configuration of the antennas. From these photographs they hoped to determine frequencies and wave length. They also expected to discern whether the stations were of German design or not.

After the mission Vic began to see the photos he'd taken on posters in every combat squadron's ready room. After that congratulatory comments from higher headquarters started rolling in. He shook many hands, and accepted with military professionalism the compliments of his superiors.

The particular type of radar he had captured on film that day, and then effectively destroyed had not been seen before. The photos showed that the enemy's technical expertise was more sophisticated than had previously been suspected. The men were told to go back for more photos, cover a wider area, and ordered not to further destroy what remained of the installation.

While Vic and his team were disappointed at the order not to completely destroy the installation, they did look forward to assisting a lightening commando raid. They flew in guns firing and camera snapping away. From above they provided cover fire for a landing party of commando's. Thanks to his previous attack on the installation, the resistance was weak.

Vic and his men flew in fast and swooped low over the crippled radar station. The commandos followed below in boats. The men wore fatigues, helmets and firm expressions. Their boots splashed in the receding water as the boats were careened onto the shore. With guns drawn and in crouched runs the men advanced on the radar station. Above, Vic drew the attention of the enemy on the ground by spewing bullets. The Japanese were too busy dodging fire from the sky that they did not suspect the commando's attack. By the time the Japanese knew of the commando presence, they had little choice but to retreat into the jungle or be shot down and left for dead.

The enemy, already weakened by the previous bombing Vic and his crew had inflicted, was dispatched with little difficulty and the facility was raided for equipment. Anything useful, informative, or just plain interesting was hauled out and loaded onto the waiting boats. Radar equipment, radios, charts, even transmissions that may prove useful upon decoding were gathered up for investigation back at base.

Rarely getting the chance to see grounds operations up close, much less such highly specialized efforts, Vic was thrilled. The excitement of a coordinated effort between land and air challenged and charged the men up. There was an extra burst of adrenaline, and a mutual respect flowed freely between the commandos and the air men.

After this, new targets and mission assignments started to come in regularly. Vic's efforts were extremely effective. Within the first three weeks of operation Vic and his team had photographed and destroyed eight Japanese early warning radars.

Typically when approaching the target, because of the secret nature of the missions and their flying in unaccompanied, the Japanese radar bases taken completely off guard. This gave Vic the upper hand in having fully loaded machine guns, before hand planning, and the advantage of the sky. Aside from small arms ground fire Vic was usually able to destroy the enemy installment quickly and come home relatively unscathed.

After receiving frag-orders for any mission, Vic would call his men together for a short briefing. They were given a location to investigate, told why the area is suspected of having early warning radar, and what kind of firepower to expect. It took only a few minutes to outline the details to the group.

The plane as a matter of course was kept ready for use at a moment's notice. The crew, pilot, co-pilot and homing equipment operator all climbed aboard and strapped in for another ride. The engines were howling for take-off as voices called out commands and last minute instructions. Adrenaline coursed its way through veins and the men were ready for take-off. It was a unique kind of thrill, different than that felt in direct combat in that it lacked the tension of kill or be killed. Knowingly going into enemy territory alone and without cover was less urgent in its danger and more like a looming threat that no one could predict. The targets they sought were deep in enemy territory. There were no fellow fighters, nor radio contact. They would come upon the Japanese installments like ghosts, armed with a camera, machine guns, and bombs. It was a thrill that few others have ever known.

They flew low and fast, hoping to evade detection and enemy fire. Coming in close to the unsuspecting Japanese encampment, Vic would drop in low over the canopy. The wind whipped the greenery back and forth, mimicking the seas that surrounded the islands. One pass-over guided by the technician and radar homing device was all they could afford for the photographs.

The men had to be efficient; they did not get second chances. After the first pass-over the enemy would have rallied itself enough to man anti-aircraft stations and begin firing. The first pass determined the precise location of the radar station and allowed Vic to snap the aerial photos that would be analyzed back on base.

He would then swing around again, his crew armed and ready, training their machine guns on the base. They returned fire for fire and refused to fall from the sky. With a command from Vic the plane released destruction from the bay doors and the men watched as the heavy metal bodies cut quietly through the air. Their forms receded, growing smaller and smaller until impact. The Earth itself was thrown up into the sky, reaching for the plane that had caused the wound. Mission completed and enemy radar destroyed the men turned again for home.

One mission took Vic and his crew to a small island off the North coast of Luzon, Cape Engano. This particular mission proved more eventful than the rest. The locals had reported that the Japanese were erecting a radar system on the island. A frag-order was issued and Vic was soon in the plane. Since he already knew where the target was located they had no need for the homing gear nor the operator, but he insisted on going along anyhow. Upon arrival the men found what they had been told to expect, a partially built radar station.

Vic flew in low, per procedure, skimming the canopy and casting shadows in the fields below. His was the only place, and this made the sound of his plane engines subtle at first. It was not until he was almost directly above the station that the enemy realized that he was coming for them. The men in the plane were ready, prepared to shoot down any adversaries, studying the radar screen for unexpected encounters, and waiting with a trained calm for the shooting to begin.

Vic dropped in lower. The soldiers on the ground, having too late realized that the plane was aimed at them, were running. Feeble attempts were made at shooting the plane down with a type 3 anti-aircraft gun and infantry machine guns. Mostly the men below were caught unprepared and had no other choice but to run.

Vic flew in as low as he could get and flipped the switch for the nose mounted camera to snap. He clicked off several pictures on the first pass, swung up and around for a second pass. This pass however was not harmless. The turret guns ripped red lines through the sky. Plumes of dust and debris rose from the ground at the semi-built structure collapsed, perforated with bullet holes. The Japanese soldiers were left stunned, wounded and thwarted as Dirty Dora II again pulled up into the sky leaving a bleeding structure behind.

After destroying the station, out of clear blue sky, a Tony appeared. Byron Reed, the co-pilot, spotted it about two o'clock high and shouted a warning. The Japanese fighter was flying parallel to Vic's plane, and exactly where it had come from was a mystery.

The usual Tony fighter tactic was to attack from about eleven o'clock high. Vic and his crew anticipated this and sure enough the plane, by then ahead of Vic's, started his turn. His intentions were clear. He intended to position himself slightly to the left and above then fire until Vic's plane was downed. Vic made the call to descend to tree top level and alerted the turret gunner.

Time slowed as the plane dropped altitude. The enemy plane cut through the sky in a graceful arc. It was quiet in the cockpit, as though the rest of the world had dropped away. The sun paused in the sky and Vic raced through the sky toward the Japanese plane. He had a firm hold of the controls but not tight. His breathing was even but a crease formed on his brow and he anticipated the moment. His crew manned their positions and waited for orders and the sound of machine-gun fire.

Vic banked to the left then looked up and saw it. Time sped up and sound returned. His engines were roaring, there was a light static on the radio headset, and there was the growing noise of the Tony engines approaching. Vic's turret guns started firing with jarring intensity. Tracers lit the path of the bullets. The Tony evaded, letting loose its own deadly fire. The missed bullets punctured the sea's surface below. Pulling up again, Vic got the other plane in his sites and lit up all twelve machine guns he carried on the nose. In spite of the amount of firepower directed at each other, the planes evaded the shots and neither was hit.

The Tony turned west and flew on with whatever mission he had been on prior to the encounter. He apparently did not realize the Vic had only moments before had destroyed the area's radar base. It had been a chance encounter and nothing more. Vic and his crew continued on and returned to base jolted through with adrenaline, pleased at the success of the mission, ready for the next, and thrilled at the chance upon encounter.

The Tank and Barn

The radar countermeasures missions covered the whole pacific theater, even as far as the coast of China. Of particular attention were northern Luzon and the adjacent Island of Samar as these islands were important Japanese strongholds in the area. One such mission took Vic to northern Luzon where a radar installment was suspected on the northern coast at Lingayan. The route to the target took the Vic's crew over the infantry advance line and put them at elevated risk of engagement, but also allowed them to witness the US ground forces at work.

En route he flew over a squadron of American soldiers held up in its advance. As he approached Vic received a radio call from the ground troop commander asking if he could help with a concealed Japanese tank. It was hidden in what looked like a barn and its fire was holding up the advance. "Of course," Vic answered.

There was more than one barn at the site and from above all of them looked alike. It took a couple of passes before the correct one was confirmed from the ground commander. Target identified Vic then pulled up to gain speed. Once he had reached an height and speed he felt were appropriate for the situation he turned and flew back in. The land below had already been punished by the tank shelling and small arms fire of the American soldiers. The grey-brown barn stood in the middle of dirt stirred up by tank tread, bullets and fire.

Vic gunned the engines and squeezed off round after round. The decimated ground sent up plumes of dust as each bullet from his nose guns dug in. The barn itself stood only a moment or two before crumpling underneath the plane's assault. A small fire ignited and Vic's attack served to feed the flames. Great streams of ammunition continued to rip through the air and decimated the tinderbox barn as the structure around the tank blossomed up then fell away like ash. The tank was silenced and riddled with smoking holes. The Japanese crew came running from the dying machine like blood.

Rid the threat to his troops and their progress the American commander from the ground radioed his thanks and set about getting his men ready to push forward. Curious to see the ground soldiers at work, Vic circled the area one more time but this time too low. He saw it in a flash just before the strike. The jeep serving as the radio vehicle, (the one that had made the call for Vic's help), had a vertical whip antenna that extended far into the air.

Vic hadn't realized he had been so low. By the time he saw the antenna registered it was too late. Adrenaline gushed through his veins, but it was not enough to pull the plane away fast enough to avoid striking. The plane hit the antenna wire rod at the wing root, missing the prop by scant inches. The plane managed to stay in the air, but the ground troop's communication was cut off. Furious with himself and humiliated Vic called off the RCM mission and returned to base expecting catastrophic damage to the airplane.

After examining the damage the crew chief expressed that he wasn't too concerned. No vital parts of the plane were hit, but the skin of the plane was cut through as if a huge knife had sliced in about eight inches. The airplane was repaired and ready for operations again in a week. And Vic was relieved the damage wasn't more extensive.

He spent that week time trying to identify the infantry unit he had "helped" to send his apologies for destroying their communications. Unfortunately it wasn't possible and he was never able to find out what had happened to them after he hit the antenna. He supposed that their advance up the island was halted as much from his curiosity as from that tank; and, in the end, he hadn't been that much help after all.

Home Building

The 499th was at San Marceline for only 5 or 6 weeks before Manila was retaken and with it the former American base at Clark Field. The move to Clark, in May of 1945, was a welcome one in that there was a real city nearby, albeit partially destroyed that still offered a retreat for war weary soldiers and pilots. There were hotel rooms with hot water, restaurants, and a few bars that remained standing after the conflict. Girls too, which was of great comfort to the men. Angeles City gave the men a taste of civilization and creature comforts that they missed terribly back on base. They missed these creature comforts so much that they sought to bring back a few of them.

Vic and a few of his officer friends decided to pool their money and employed a Filipino crew to build a house. It was built mostly of bamboo and included two bedrooms, a kitchen, and a living room. Best of all there was a shower. A P-40 belly tank served as the water tank. It was suspended over a raised slatted floor and the water fed through a perforated coffee can. The place was pure luxury and the envy of the entire base.

Sunlight filtered through gaps in the bamboo walls while the smell of dust and tropical fruit ripening on the trees of the jungle wafted through the air. In the kitchen there was no sink, running water, or even real cabinets. The only furniture was a metal table that stood prominent in the center of the room with four chairs around it, a side table where food was prepared, and a refrigerator that didn't work.

The largest room, serving as living room, had two large shuttered windows that stood open for the majority of the day. Chairs that had been salvaged from the previously abandoned base offices sat on the rough hewn floors. Footsteps echoed in this room and voices were always loud, but this only added to the relaxed nature of the place. In each of the two bedrooms there were two or three cots. Not much in the way of home comfort, but extreme luxury when compared to sleeping in foxholes or dirt floored tents under a tropical deluge.

The roof was made of hollow bamboo shafts lashed together and was musical in the rain. The average temperature of the shaded home was at least ten degrees cooler than outside and made an easy living arrangement that was nearly impossible to find on any military field base.

The Squadron Engineering Officer, Ed Egan, had "liberated" the refrigerator on one of his forays into Manila. It was a large gas powered thing, but of course there was no gas to be had. Ed thought it could be converted to electric. He felt that with both his and Vic's engineering education it should be a simple enough task.

It made quite the comedy with the Squadron Engineering Officer and Radar Counter Measures Officer poking around the base scrounging for scrap-electric wire and odd pieces. Sweating and shirtless in the afternoon heat the two men bent over the dead refrigerator trying to wind scrap wire into a coil. It was this hand-made coil that they intended to mount in the gas burner of the refrigerator to use for power. Their hands were blackened from working the metal and removing the old gas parts--a large heap of cast off metal bits to one side, making a graveyard of failed attempts. Their two faces floated close together as they fought with stubborn screws, cooling cores and resisting wire coils. Sweat, swears, and sunburns were all that would ever be gained and the house never had a working fridge.

Destroying a Destroyer

After several weeks at Clark Field the number of targets for radar counter measures grew fewer and fewer. The heavy bomber crews reported much reduced early warning Japanese defense activity and Vic felt a sense of accomplishment. The results of his time and effort were proved justified and had made a marked impact. His superiors at Section 22 evidently thought so too, as he was recommended for a second DFC (Distinguished Flying Cross).

In July the 345th was relocated to Ie Shima, where Vic continued with his Radar Countermeasures work. The missions continued on through August and into Sept of 1945. Vic and his crew had destroyed many enemy radar installations but eventually the forays dried up. They had evidentially destroyed all the installations in the area. He and his crew had conducted 33 "Radar Busting" missions and destroyed 16 Japanese installations. These included: 1 on Catanduanes Island, 9 on Luzon, 3 on Formosa, and 3 on the China Coast. These missions included photography, bombing and strafing, and engaging what enemy planes managed to intercept Dirty Dora II--all conducted alone and without the support of a flight group. It had been exciting and successful. It was so successful in fact that Vic had again begun to feel his talents being wasted and eventually decided he wanted out of the radar assignment.

He wrote a proposal to be reattached as a member in good standing of the 345th Bomb Group of the 499th Squadron, while keeping his plane available if the need arose for future Radar Countermeasure works. His superiors at 5th Air Force agreed readily enough to transfer him back to the Squadron as a bomber pilot and on September 26th, 1945, Vic was again a bomber pilot with the Air Apaches and appointed as a flight leader.

Not only were radar installation targets dwindling, so too were active enemy engagements and Japanese resistance. In response the U.S. forces began to focus more on convoys and preventing Japanese military resurgence. These convoys were merchant ships and destroyers, en-route to what remained of the Japanese bases with weapons, medical supplies, food, and reinforcements. When U.S. intelligence would get word of a convoy, U.S. formations would be sent out to intercept and sink them. The intended result was to starve out of the isolated Japanese ground forces.

After a successful bomb run to tenderize the already weakened area, Vic and his formation came across one such convoy. They were fresh out of bombs but all the men were loath to let the opportunity pass. As they approached the Japanese supply ships and destroyer Vic radioed out for the squadron to take out the entire convoy. He gave quick instructions on which planes were to take which targets and set to work.

Vic instructed his wing man to sweep the decks of the destroyer and eliminate the threat of the on deck anti-aircraft guns. He would then swoop in and open up a storm of machine gun fire and hopefully sink or cripple the ship.

The Japanese saw the planes coming and scrambled to positions on deck, hoping to fend them off or at the very least knock a couple out of the sky. Fortunately for Vic and his flight group, they had the element of surprise and were more prepared for the attack then the Japanese had been.

The planes cast deadly shadows on the waters below, and the Japanese ships made easy targets. Across the decks Japanese navy and merchant men scrambled for cover. Deck mounted anti-aircraft guns fired desperately into the air, but the U.S. planes refused to be downed.

The air roared with plane engines, machine gun fire, and anti-aircraft fire from the deck guns. The water churned away beneath the behemoths as the engines of the giant ships worked to pull them away from the agile planes. The sky belayed the danger and played host to puffed clouds and bright sunshine as B-25's swooped in and fired on the slow metal leviathans. Machine gun fire tore through ship decks, rendered useless the anti-aircraft guns, and set fuel supplies ablaze. Fatal wounds bled air into the sea, and flooded lower levels dragged the leviathans down from the surface. The groans of broken and dying ships echoed through the water. Men were trapped within the bodies of the dying beasts while others struggled into life boats and kicked away from the under tow.

    Vic's assault on the destroyer was successful. While his wingman strafed the deck to eliminate threat of deck guns, Vic punched a massive hole into the side of the destroyer then pulled up. The ship sank slowly, the water surrounding it bubbling up air and men. He had taken out an entire destroyer with machine gun fire alone and suffered no losses. It had been a successful mission that led to a valuable surprise encounter, and letter of commendation made it into Vic's file.

End of Hostilities

Through the summer of 1945 the number of targets reachable from Clark Field diminished and the intensity of enemy encounters slackened. Everybody in the Pacific Theater could see the writing on the wall; the war was nearing an end. The Philippines had been retaken, the Okinawa operation had been bloody but successful, and Japan itself was being destroyed by forces on Okinawa, Ie Shima, Guam, and Tinian. With each victory U.S. troops pushed further into Japanese waters.

Forced to follow the ever moving conflict zones, Vic and his compatriots were loath to leave the lovely house that had been built for them at Clark Field. They had even employed a house boy and laundry girl. But it wasn't meant to last. After the Okinawa Campaign at the end of June they were ordered to move north to Ie Shima, a little island just off Okinawa. The 345th was fully established by early July and it was there, in Ie Shima, that he began his bombing missions again.

He flew missions targeting shipping lanes for cargo and troopships, enemy fighter planes, and even the Japanese home islands. Attention had shifted from just beating Japanese forces off of occupied islands to overtaking Japan itself. Planning and preparation was now centered on the timing of an invasion of the Japanese islands. Then came August 6, 1945, the day Hiroshima and then Nagasaki were both destroyed. This was the day when humanity unleashed an encapsulated power with the potential to destroy mountain ranges and reduce entire populations to ash.

After the bombs had been dropped enemy activity stopped and U.S. planes performed little more than fly-over for confirmation of a crippled enemy. Vic's last few missions of the war were executed over Japan proper. He was to locate any possible enemy threat and eliminate it. The missions were milk runs really, not much activity, no return fire, nor really any movement on the ground at all. There were no people, military or civilian, in the streets; nor cars on the roads.

All was an ash grey and barren landscape that swept along underneath the cockpit of Vic's plane. The growl of the engines was the only sound for miles; and his very shadow cast down from the sky, was the only movement. Vic's attention stayed sharp and his eyes scanned ahead. He was too familiar with the surprises of war and knew that even in such dead stillness enemy threat could still lurk like a wounded animal.

On one such desolate mission, on August 14 or 15 depending on which side of the date line you were on, Vic and his men were called back before reaching the target. The mission was called off in route and that was enough to know a cease fire had been called. Mid flight, on the way to one more mission, one more exchange of gunfire, one more reconnaissance mission scanning for enemy activity, after almost four years of war, it was over.

In the cockpit the radio crackled into life. The squad had been flying for less than an hour, their muscles had already relaxed into the motion of the plane and their bones hummed along with the engines that held them aloft: Perfect formation, as always, smooth flying, with Vic in the lead. He had briefed the men on the target, on what sort of encampment they were looking for, and the reports of activity. Each pilot, navigator and gunman was prepared and ready for yet another mission over the dying land of Japan.

Radio communication was short and direct. These men had flown together long enough not to need second and third instructions. Orders were clear and expectations understood. Vic would have needed little more than to say to his men, "Let's go," and it would be done. They were focused, attentive, and ready. Save for the roar of the plane engines, it would have been quiet. Then static scratched through the headset followed by code names and a single order.

"The mission has been canceled. Return to base. Repeat; return to base."

Without a second thought Vic confirmed and ordered his men to turn around. They had flown over the edge of the war and into an uneasy peace. There were no shouts of triumph, no sobs of grief or gratitude, just curt orders and a sharp bank to the left to return home. They were all going home and very much aware of it.

In the days after the cease fire, the military turned its attention to the P.O.W. camps and missing soldiers. The war had seen the establishment of many cruel and often deadly war camps. Prisoners were subjected to beatings, starvation, and isolation. Soldiers not only died from horrendous human cruelty, they also suffered and wasted away from dysentery and infection in those jungle camps. During the cease fire Vic flew over P.O.W. camps in Formosa and Japan. He and the rest of his bomb group dropped food and clothing to allied prisoners, and helped transport survivors who were found in battle worn areas.

Flying in over the P.O.W. camps Vic dropped bundles much like those he had dropped on the biscuit bombing runs when he was still new to the war. Large canvas packages, bound up tightly, contained food, blankets, clothing and medical gear. It was an incomparable relief to those worn and weary men who had been so long locked up in muddy camps living off scraps and dirty water to receive those life saving bundles.

Of course the men waiting in the camps did not immediately know that a cease fire had been called. They would have expected bombs and machine gun fire to burst forth from the planes that raced in overhead. Bodies tensing as they watched their brothers in arms come in hot and release from the bellies of the planes small dark shapes that dropped with the same speed as any bomb. As the parachute buoyed package made their descent they belayed the threat of bombing. Relief and gratitude would have washed over the starving men realizing that the drops were intended to ease their suffering rather than add to it.

General MacArthur's cease fire demand included a stipulation that required the Japanese air base at Atsugi be made immediately available for U.S. aircraft and personnel. In the days leading up to the turnover of the base, a daily photo reconnaissance mission was undertaken. These reconnaissance missions told U.S. officials when the base was truly accessible and kept all those involved up to date on progress. It was now just a matter of waiting.

With the guns of war silenced and the air stilled of war plane propellers, the smoke began to clear revealing vast stretches of land pulverized and charred. The destruction from the atomic bombs over Hiroshima and Nagasaki had left the bustling hills and valleys of the burgeoning metropolis desolate and a barren black.

It was rumored that these two great cities of Japan had evaporated in the bombing. The men of Vic's squadron could not believe the reports. How could one bomb erase an entire city? It was true that each of these men had flown over towns and villages where enemy strongholds had been ensconced while carrying enough firepower to obliterate an entire settlement. It was true too, that they had effectively destroyed those strongholds when their orders had called on them to do so. But never had a single bomb bay door released enough destructive power to eliminate everything at a target. It took ten to twelve planes with full machine gun fire and dozens of bombs to pepper the land below. Even then, the range of destruction and chaos was limited. The sort of destructive power reputed to been wrecked on Nagasaki and Hiroshima was something that had to be seen to believe.

During the quiet, Vic and the grounds officers he lived with decided to take the opportunity to see for themselves what the impact of those bombs looked like. Vic took multiple trips carrying many of the long time ground officers to see the devastation that was Hiroshima and Nagasaki, as well as the burned out Tokyo. They flew a scant twenty feet above the ash covered ground. No one had informed the men of the risks of radiation, or the health consequences such exposure could have. Even had they been aware of the risks they would still have been compelled to see it with their own eyes.

The ground was gray dirt in some areas, melted glass in others. Improbable skeletons of trees ringed the outermost reaches of the bombs explosion. The cities themselves, which had once served as home to thousands, were all gone. There was not a single building left standing. The ruins of the cities were no more than piles of dirt and ruble that stretched for miles. A few buildings on the outskirts left little more than charred bones and steel framing that stood as a grisly reminder.

Prior to the atomic drops Tokyo had suffered a month's long series of air raids and bombings. The result was a beleaguered and nearly decimated city coated in ash and rubble. Vic flew men to see the ruins of this great city as well. The once proud city of Tokyo was yet another smoking ruin in a war that spread destruction and loss across the entire world.

Flying so close and low over crushed buildings, lost lives, and abandoned dreams was surreal. There was only sorrow made manifest in ash, and the city's charred remains gave no sense of hope or life. Improbably, in Tokyo, the Emperor's palace was an island of green in a sea of gray dust. Somehow during those months of air raids with hundreds of bombs and machine gun fire spewing across the city, the palace had been spared. It took incredible precision on the part of the B-29 pilots and bombardiers to leave that small plot unscathed. On that floating island of green sat the last shining emblem of hope for recovery.

One such sightseeing trip Vic flew with the squadron Engineering Officer, Ed Egan. The two marveled at the destruction and whistled through their teeth in awe before turning back for base. As they flew over dancing open water, perhaps in order to erase the unease that had settled over him, Egan asked how fast a B-25 could fly wide open. Vic responded by pointing to the red line on the airspeed indicator, which topped out at 280 MPH.

"But how fast, really, will it go?" Ed asked.

Vic really couldn't answer. The only thing the manual said was that maximum power could be held for two minutes and he'd never exceeded that limit. Egan thought about this for less than a second before suggesting they find out what the true highest speed was. When they landed at Ie Shima he instructed the crew chief to have the airplane stripped.

Ed ordered the plane stripped of its camouflage paint right down to shiny aluminum. The personnel removed all combat equipment: the turret with its guns, ammo tracks and magazines, all armor plate, both bomb racks, and side gun packs. Even the gun wiring harness was removed. Then the radar electronics gear was removed and packed for shipment. The sheet metal people covered all the newly exposed openings with new metal sheets. In the end Dirty Dora II was made a new plane. She shone in the sun, as sleek and elegant as she had when first manufactured.

After the work was complete Egan called Vic to say the airplane was ready for the test. They climbed aboard and flew out over the water. Vic chose to hold about twenty feet over the water and opened her up.

The two men encapsulated in aluminum raced like a streak of silver light over an expanse of ever moving turquoise. The two men grinned with gritted teeth, thrilled and fierce in the pursuit of ever greater speed. They raced on challenging the waves to a race to the horizon. Above them, wind-swept clouds stretched out in a failed attempt to join in: Azure above, turquoise below with silver tearing a straight line between the two. Faster and faster they flew. Their backs were forced into their seats as they reached a top speed of to 325 MPH, and answered Ed Egan's question.

The Surrender

During the cease fire the Operations Officer of the squadron, Jim Banks, informed the men that a delegation had been called to represent the Japanese government. This delegation was to be sent, via Ie Shima, to Manila where they were to discuss the details of the Japanese surrender with General MacArthur's staff. They would travel from Tokyo in two specially marked BETTY bombers, twin engine Mitsubishi bombers that the Japanese had used throughout the war. The BETTY's would land at the airstrip in Ie Shima where the delegation would then transfer to two C-54s that would take them on to Manila. The delegation was to be escorted during the trip by two B-25s of the 345th Bomb Group (Vic's group), one from the 498th and one from the 499th

At noon on day of negotiations, the delegation had arrived with their escort of B-25's at Ie Shima. Each plane landed safely and without incident and the transfer took place. With the Delegation safely ensconced in the official C-54's, they took to the sky, and headed South to Manila. The Bettys and their pilots however, were to remain at Ie Shima for the delegates return flight to Tokyo once the negations were completed.

After the delegation team left, the Bettys were given a quick look over by the base mechanics. It was a fortunate thing too, as several mechanical problems were found. Had they gone unnoticed the planes may not have made it back to Tokyo at all. Repairs were started immediately by the Japanese crew and in an odd twist of circumstance several of the U.S. mechanics were recruited to help.

A few weeks prior it would have been unthinkable that these men fighting on opposing sides of the war would cram their heads and hands together into the same oily plane engine for repairs. They worked, grunted, and laughed together ensuring the planes were in tip-top shape so that the Japanese crews would make it home safely. How odd an experience it must have been for them to work together?

One of the planes was still being repaired when the delegation returned and so was not ready for flight. Negotiations complete, the delegation returned to Ie Shima where they were divided into two groups. One group was to take the functional airplane back to Tokyo and the second would wait for the repairs to be completed to follow the second day.

The first group was led by the head of the delegation, LT. General Torashiro Kanabe, Vice Chief of the Army General Staff. The general and his group boarded the flyable airplane with the documents ready for presentation to the Japanese Emperor. These documents laid out instructions and procedures for the upcoming surrender and hand over of all Japanese holdings in the Pacific. Among the requirements the Japanese government was to provide accommodations for the U.S. military, harbor Facilities at Yokahama, and the airfield at Atsugi. The Japanese government and military were to expect the arrival of the initial Allied forces and there was to be a reception of the Allied Occupation to welcome the American officials.

It was August 20, 1945, when the Japanese Betty planes left Ie Shima carrying papers laying out the terms of peace. It had been four years since Vic had joined the U.S. Army Air Corps, four years of excitement, boredom, terror, and the beginning of many life-long friendships. He stood beside the taxi strip alongside roughly 500 others watching the engines of the first Betty start. He, like so many, watched the plane take off, carrying with it the hopes and relief of every service man in the Philippines, both Japanese and Allied.

Watching the first plane of the Japanese delegates return to Japan, Vic heaved a great sigh of relief, but also felt a measure of anxiety. He asked himself, "What now? What's next in my life? A chapter, no, a whole book had just ended. What would the next volume bring?"

With the first half of the Japanese delegation en route to Japan along with the American escort planes, a second escort team needed to be assembled for the remaining plane. Vic was assigned to lead this flight. He and his crew were briefed and prepared for the flight to Tokyo. The following day found the men ready and eager to take off. The crew for this flight was not Vic's normal crew but one that was made of up specific people who deserved the honor. They were the old timers, the grounds people who had been in the squadron since its activation three years before. These men had served with distinction, weathered the parading from base to base, sent the notification of deaths back to families, survived the loss of so many friends, and watched the whole of the war from first hand perspectives.

That morning Vic took to the sky as smooth and clean as ever then circled around as the Japanese plane lifted off. The planes joined up then headed toward Tokyo. On the way Vic couldn't help but think of the irony of it all. There he was, seeing to the safety of a bunch of Japanese officials when only a week before, any of either group would have freely killed the members of the other.

The flight from Ie Shima to Tokyo was uneventful and quiet. The water passed beneath them and seemed less turbulent than it had on previous flights. The sunlight glinted, cheery and playful, up at the plane as it would perhaps to a sailor out for a pleasure cruise. It was a relief after the years of conflict and threat of being shot down at any time to look down at the water and appreciate its beauty rather than scan for targets or threats.

The escort formation saw the Japanese plane safely to the mainland then turned for home. Behind him was the descending plane of a recent enemy turned ally. Before him was the return flight, the first of peacetime. Vic found himself still scanning for enemy ships and thinking of his original crew. They were now all safe back home in the States, or had crossed the veil. Vic was proud to be in the company of the men who had earned the honor of this flight, but he couldn't help thinking of how his original group would have enjoyed this brief flight, all together again, flying the final mission of a terrible bloody war.

Shortly after seeing the Japanese delegates safely back to their homeland the official surrender signing ceremony occurred on September 2. Four days later Vic was told he was to lead a flight of six airplanes to Kimpo Airfield (then called by its Japanese name, Keijo) to carry general Hodge and his staff to accept the formal Japanese surrender of Korea. The flight was made up of two elements. Three airplanes for each element were to fly to Okinawa to pick up their passengers on September 7, 1945.

The honor of flying this surrender mission was again reserved for those who had served with distinction. Vic had twice earned the honor of the Distinguished Flying Cross, served more than one tour, been responsible for the implementation and over-seeing of the successful radar countermeasures program, and served hundreds of hours of combat flying. He had a glowing record and was more than deserving of the honor of leading the surrender flight.

The flight from Ie Shima to Kimpo was not a terribly long one, but it was perhaps the single most important flight he was ever to make. When they arrived at Kimpo Airdrome, which had previously been a Japanese fighter base, he could see that the landing runway was too short for the B-25s. There was a lot riding on this flight and the landing had to be clean. Vic took in the situation as he flew over and decided that before allowing the General's plane to risk a short landing, he would have to ensure the safety of it himself.

He flew in low over the swath of packed dirt serving as runway. He did not land but instead flew over to approximate its length. He flew in so low that he nearly grazed the ground and as he pulled up a plume of dust was stirred up. He shook his head in displeasure at the abbreviated landing strip, but was unwilling to let this momentous landing be thwarted. Gaining the sky again he sent out a call over the radio telling his flight group to circle the airfield while he attempted the landing. More than one man whistled incredulously at the prospect and watched as Vic descended again toward the landing site.

By keeping the airspeed as slow as possible and touching down at the very far edge of the runway threshold, Vic figured he could probably do it. Probably is of course not the same thing as certainty. His decent was slow and controlled and the ground approached as though it were hesitant to meet the plane. At the very edge of the runway the plane grazed the grass and touched down as soft as a caress.

The instant his tires touched the surface Vic stood full weight on the brakes. The abrupt decline in speed was jarring compared to the gentleness of the touchdown. Despite the force applied to the brakes, the plane nearly flew down the full length of the tarmac. The assembled and waiting Japanese soldiers whipped by in a blur on one side of the tarmac. On the other, Japanese war planes with their signature red circles and war weathered buildings rushed away as Vic continued to race down the runway.

The edge of the runway rushed towards him: 2,000 feet, 1,000 feet, 750 feet, 500 feet. He pushed down harder still on the brakes. He sucked in a frustrated breath and scanned the brush ahead of him to pick out his line: 500 feet, slower, 450 ft, slower, 400 ft, slower, 350 ft, and slower still. The edge of the packed runway that had been screaming at him was now getting closer at a manageable speed. He rolled to a stop at the far end of the runway mere feet from the edge. It was a tricky landing to pull off, but he had managed to land safely and knew what was necessary for the rest of his flight to do the same.

He radioed his instructions to the still circling flight group. He then watched as one by one of the planes; following his orders, each approached and landed without incident on the dramatically short runway. He refused to let any hesitation show on his face as each plane made its initial contact with the ground and strained to slow in time to avoid careening off the runway into the brush. It would have been unseemly for an American bomber pilot to have looked nervous in front of the defeated Japanese forces. It would have been even more so for an American plane to go headlong off the Japanese runway.

After each plane had landed, the flight engineer managed the parking of the airplanes. He lined them up with exacting precision, wing tip to wing tip. While this would have been procedure at any landing, the flight engineer took special care: this time due less to procedure and more to make an impression on the Japanese troops watching.

The planes having landed safely and now under the capable hands of the engineer, Vic shifted his attention to the assembly that had gathered for the event. It seemed to him that the whole Japanese 3rd Division, fully armed, was standing at attention in front of the terminal building. Hundreds of Japanese soldiers returned Vic's level gaze. While not exactly staring at him, it felt like it; for, these men, only days before, had simply been the enemy. Now assembled and waiting for an American General to emerge from a plane, these same men had suddenly become human.

Disembarking from the plane General Hodge assembled his staff in the parking area and walked smartly to just in front of the enemy troops. He exchanged salutes with the Japanese commander, who presented his sword to the general. As a sign of mutual respect and compassion General Hodge refused the sword saying he hoped it would never be drawn in anger again. The meeting ceremony thus concluded, the troops were marched off and the representatives of the two governments went into the building.

Vacation in Seoul

After delivering the General and his delegation to the official surrender ceremony and negotiations, Vic and the men turned their attention to the planes, closing them up and seeing that they were parked and ready for the return flight. Just as they finished several trucks drove up. The men loaded up and were driven to downtown Seoul where luxurious rooms were waiting for them in The Chosen Hotel. As the leader of the group, Vic was given a suite fit for a king, a far cry from the tent he had left back at Ie Shima. The hotel people addressed him with his name and rank. How they knew who he was baffled him.

It had been intended that Vic and his flight group return the next day to Okinawa and then the base at Ie Shima. But, in light of how dangerously bright the sun was and how terribly shaded the spaces under the palm trees were he decided the weather was simply too bad for safe flying. So, he radioed headquarters to apprise them of the situation and hoped the group's weather people couldn't see all the way to Korea.

The men were assigned two whole floors for their quarters. There were soft beds with clean sheets, a luxury not afforded at Ie Shima where the men slept on cots in canvas tents that did little more than keep the worst of the torrential downpours off a body. Standing at the window in his room and looking out on the now peaceful Seoul, Vic sighed wistfully at the luxury that surrounded him.

Amidst the luxury of running water, fresh linens, and window curtains, the men ran into one major problem in paradise. There was almost no food. The stores of the city had dwindled to nearly nonexistent during the war and much of the nation was starving. The Japanese supply ships that the U.S. had worked so hard to prevent from reaching the Japanese military were also prevented from reaching civilians. This was one of the hard facts of war, for those in power to be over thrown or defeated those without are made to suffer. The elderly, children, and men and women who wished only peace were the unlucky victims.

Being guests of hosts with nothing to offer, for three days, the men ate nothing but apples and what little might be bartered for with cigarettes. Aside from munching hungrily on apples that never quite hit the bottom of a growling stomach, life was grand in the plush hotel. The men lounged on soft cushions and chatted up friendly hotel staff. Leisurely strolls through the quiet hotel gardens offered a stark contrast to hearing war machines rip through the sky.

Japanese officials rushed to and fro in the hotel lobby. Local people mingled in the quiet sunshine of the afternoons, and two formerly opposing military uniforms could be spotted around the hotel. Everyone moved about as though in a dream, not really believing that the world could be so quite or so bright. Everyone waited for the lie to be exposed, that the war was not really over. Three days passed in a strange surreal blissfulness of relaxation and hunger hazed consciousness.

During the men's stay in Seoul Vic was approached several times by various political group representatives. The men, who came calling, asked that he use his influence as an honored colleague of General MacArthur to help seat one representative or another at the take-over administration. One of the politicians pleaded with him to intercede with General MacArthur and suggested that Syngman Rhee be awarded the presidency. Since Vic was apparently the leader of such a mighty air force, he certainly had the ear of General MacArthur. The politicians couldn't believe that Vic was just the bus driver with no power in appointing heads of state. Oddly enough, it did follow that Syngman Rhee did become Korea's first elected president without Vic's direct influence.

The encounters were amusing and embarrassing for Vic. Lounging and laughing with his men and their apples, their voices bounced off the stone patios of the hotel, theirs the only rolling around with joviality. All the delegates were in conferences discussing terms of surrender, proposing supported governments, and lining out the endless details that consume such people at the cessation of war. Vic and his men however, indulged in the tranquility of a quiet hotel with eager staff in a city that no longer vibrated with the sounds of war planes and naval assault.

The newly organized politicians of Seoul approached quietly, emerging into the sunshine from the darkened hotel with seeming timidity. The pilots were dressed in flight suits and joked good-naturedly together. A soft click of fine shoes scuffed from years of living bowed to Japanese occupation would have gained the ears of Vic and his men and caused them to turn toward the sound with curiosity.

American smiles and a few pleased-as-punch apple crunches welcomed the somewhat hesitant Koreans wearing hopeful expressions and faded suits. The approaching men stopped to bow at the waist and Vic stood. He nodded, unsure of what to expect. Were these men bringing communication from his superiors? Was he needed for piloting more delegates to an emergency meeting on another base? Or perhaps these suited men were simply curious about American service-men.

Vic's face reflected his curiosity with a raised eye brow and a still mouth that shifted to a toothy grinning expression of shock when he learned he was thought to be a man of power. Vic stumbled over his thoughts while earnest looking Korean politicians and activists stood before him smiling and insisting on the justification of their cause. Surprised and a little uncomfortable, Vic laughed politely. His surprise gave way to embarrassment at having to correct these men in their understanding.

He patiently heard out each of their pleas and suggestions on who should be recommended for the new presidency and endeavored to help the nervous men feel at ease by looking attentively at each face as they spoke. He nodded his concern and acknowledged their worries before responding that if he had the authority he would have their concerns considered, but as it stood he held no such power. It took a little convincing for a few of them that Vic was just a pilot and not a U.S. dignitary who had the ear of General MacArthur.

With a smile full of pride, amusement, and a little humility he found it hard explain that he had merely brought the general and the international delegation and had not in fact come with them. Nor did he hold any sway in the great decisions that were being made. He felt sympathy for the men who had beseeched him and was honored to have been found, albeit inaccurately, to have such powerful political clout and associates.

In spite of having been mistaken for a leader of the great American Air Force, Vic made the best of his few days of rest. The weather he had fabricated lifted after three days and it came time for the men to head back to Ie Shima.

The trip back to base was uneventful and this gave Vic plenty of time to worry about his predicament. He had after all hi-jacked six airplanes and twenty five men. As the island got closer and closer Vic's imagined a courts martial. The closer the island got the more vivid became his imaginings. All the benefit of the rest and relaxation in Seoul was undone on the flight back to base. The planes landed clean and quick and Vic pulled into place. As he was shutting down the airplane, with the engine still warm and headset on. A jeep drove up to Vic's window.

"You're to come with me immediately sir," the driver said, "To report to the Ops Officer."

Vic's stomach sank. His face, normally firm and confident, would have let slip a single twitch of a grimace almost too small to detect. His brows pitched towards one another and an exhale of resignation whooshed from his nostrils and he nodded his head. Arriving in the office of the Ops Officers, Vic found a furious Lt. Colonel Max Mortison.

"How dare you pull a stupid stunt like that; I should throw the book at you."

"Really bad weather sir. I certainly didn't want to jeopardize the men. Since many of the pilots in the flight were relatively inexperienced, to take those pilots into that kind of weather... Well I just couldn't risk it."

"Yeah, right."

The man's pique was understandable; Vic had kept six airplanes and their crews away from base just to enjoy the clean sheets and hot showers of civilization for three days. He understood, but didn't really feel too bad about it. The Lt. Colonel, though angry, could do very little to reprimand Vic and could not prove that he hadn't acted with the men's safety at heart. To add insult to injury, Lt. Colonel Max Mortison had to stand by and watch while Vic was awarded afterwards with another Distinguished Flying Cross for, "...organizing and carrying out a program to locate and destroy enemy early warning radar, thereby saving lives and aircraft of the United States Army Air Force. He, personally, with a crew of volunteers, flew his specially equipped aircraft, alone and without fighter escort protection, into enemy controlled airspace to carry out this hazardous mission, which he did with exemplary success."

Stranded

After the successful surrender of Japan and its territories U.S. troops began receiving return orders, and returning home. Men around the theater waited with little patience to receive orders of their own. Each day the men woke hopeful that their papers of release from the bondage of war would come.

The return of the troops to the U.S. began haphazardly at the end of September 1945 and it was mass chaos. Thousands of men stood by waiting for release papers. Planes and ships were overwhelmed with transport responsibilities and loaded every day to capacity with men and goods leaving the Pacific. Men stacked one upon another on the transports. Headquarters struggled to keep things in order, and even when running smoothly evacuations were hectic and chaotic. There was an ever present backlog of men awaiting their turn to head home. But gradually people were shipped home. The old war planes were either destroyed or sent to Japan for the occupation forces, and the world as a whole began to heal.

It took a month of waiting and anticipating that coveted return-to-the-States order before it occurred to Vic that the fastest was back was to fly his own airplane. His airplane had been stripped down weeks earlier by Ed Eagan and his crew when the two had decided to find out how fast the plane could fly. Vic spoke with the Squadron Commander, Wendell Decker, who told Vic that all airplanes in the theater were to be held in position until the "wheels" determined what was needed for the coming occupation of Japan. He was officially not allowed to use his plane and was supposed to stay put until told otherwise.

Knowing Vic's agitation to do something, Decker made a suggestion, "Go see General Crabb, maybe he'll grant an exception."

General Crabb was the Commanding General of the 5th

Bomber Command. He had been the Group Commander in the early days and Vic hoped to be remembered. He made an appointment and flew over to Okinawa to the general's headquarters. Unfortunately, the trip was a bust and Vic was informed that the hold order had come from General Kenny, and the issue was out of the Crabb's hands.

It was a disappointment and a hard blow. Vic had already started planning the trip: Hong Kong, through the Malay States, and on to India. He planned to stop in Egypt; then go on through Europe and cross the North Atlantic. The smells of exotic spices and the taste of mint tea lingered in his imagination even after the disappointment settled into the routine of life on base in the quiet after war.

It was during this quiet that Wendell Decker introduced Vic to a one star General. The men met in Decker's office with the sunlight filtering between slatted windows. The sounds of heavy boots on dirt pack, mechanics tinkering, and men's voices hung low in the tropical heat outside of the office. Vic stood at attention before Decker and the General.

"The General wants to see your airplane."

"Damn," Vic thought, "This is somehow connected to the speed run with Egan, or perhaps to the Korea episode."

He could feel the ass chewing that was coming, his stomach tightened and his spine braced for the verbal onslaught. But rather than reaming into Vic about procedure and conduct the General politely followed Vic to the plane. There wasn't a mark on Dirty Dora, nor was there anything wrong with her, so what the General could have wanted to see Vic had no idea.

Outside, the two men climbed into the General's jeep. Vic was silent and the General was disinclined to make conversation, the driver drove to the flight line where Vic and the General climbed out. Vic indicated his plane and watched as his superior walked around the airplane, climbed in, and inspected the flight deck. He asked about the alterations for single pilot operation. Vic told him what the modifications were, to which the General nodded and nothing else said.

They drove back to Wendell's office and Vic mulled over the possibilities that would have caught the attention of the General. Perhaps it wasn't the speed run. Then again, perhaps it was. If it was, how had the man found out, and how bad was the reprimand going to be? Vic took the silence as confirmation of trouble coming. He wondered what the hell this whole thing was all about. Back in Decker's office Vic stood erect with his eyes forward, waiting.

"I'll take the airplane. Have all the squadron gear removed and I'll send my crew around tomorrow to fly it to my headquarters."

Vic's jaw dropped. He felt the tropical heat dissipate with the chilly realization of immediate loss. He was betrayed by rank and the way things worked. His airplane, the one that had carried him over so many miles of enemy territory safely, the one that had born him aloft over exploding oceans where battling navies mixed blood with salt water, the plane that he loved and touched with the same tenderness he would touch woman, was gone just like that. He stood open mouthed and flabbergasted. How could this happen? That was HIS airplane.

The next day he watched as the General's crew started up and taxied out. He stood grim faced, rigid with loss, shock and anger. His teeth clenched against vocalizing futile emotions and watched Dirty Dora II for the last time. Standing there powerless to prevent the surprisingly personal loss he realized that the war was truly over at last.

With his plane taken and no return papers issued Vic, with the rest of the men, was stranded at Ie Shima. With the sudden end of hostilities that caught everyone by surprise the program to return troops to the states was never fully organized. The Navy and Merchant Marine troop transport ships were still hauling people and supplies to the theater for a continuing war even after the surrender had been signed. To make the situation worse, the people who directed troop and supply movements– primarily the Quartermaster Corps in Washington– were in the midst of reorganizing and still preparing for the Japanese home island invasion.

Further exacerbating the situation, a terrible typhoon swept through the Pacific in October, which took out lines of communication and stalled all transport into and out of the Pacific. Men with return orders were stranded in bases around the theater. Damage to remote bases from the typhoon left food supplies contaminated, medical supplies in short supply, and no there was no way of securing relief or extraction for weeks. In the helter-skelter of re-grouping after the storm entire bases were forgotten resulting transport ferries and re-supply shipments that stopped coming. The base at Ie Shima was one such base.

Being on the far end of the line they had been low on the list of priorities in the first place. Luckily plenty of supplies were on hand and there was enough to last them for months if necessary. So it was, from the end of September to the beginning of November of 1945, Vic and his compatriots lived peacefully in a tropical haze of military confusion and obscurity.

In early November, the removal of personnel ratcheted up a notch and Ie Shima began received return orders. Troop ships were waiting in Okinawa ports and those who had been in theater longest began receiving orders to report to the embarkation point. The men were officially going home and elated. There was a problem though: someone forgot to arrange ferries to Okinawa. Their airplanes had been transferred to the 38th Bomb Group which was part of the occupation force, so the men of the 499th and 345th couldn't leave the island. Even Vic's plane had been taken by the general. All this left them truly stranded with dwindling supplies and patchy communication from the already overworked head offices at Naha. Their cries for relief and evacuation transport went unheeded.

In an effort to get men home, it was discovered that one of the units also based on Ie Shima was a liaison squadron that flew Piper Cubs (L-4s). These, like the planes of Vic's group, had been re-assigned to the occupation force and shipped out a week or so after the surrender. Fortunately, as fate would have it one Cub had been left behind.

Considering the situation, lack of communication and the ease in which their group had been forgotten the Squadron Armament Officer, Bob Post, and Vic decided to "requisition" the Cub. They would make it flyable and fly it over to Okinawa. They wanted to talk face to face with whoever had the authority to arrange for ferrying people from Ie Shima.

Late one evening, a group of them dragged the little airplane from the other unit to their own encampment--all very hush-hush. The mechanics had the engine running by daylight. Vic and Bob were airborne by 0900 hours.

In little more than an hour they landed at Naha where FEAF (the Far East Air Force) offices and headquarters was based. The place was teeming with people and ran at a low level of chaos. Men all around them were too busy to look up, others were simply too dazed from exhaustion to be of much help. Eventually Vic and Bob were able to locate the office of the Commanding General. They had decided to go directly to the top and bypass the overworked underlings that had thus far not been able to arrange the proper transport for their group.

Of course they were turned away at the office and redirected to an underling in the Chief of Staff's office. They related the plight of those left on Ie Shima to whomever would listen and after numerous retellings they finally met an officer on the staff of the Chief of Ground Transportation. Due to his confusion it was instantly clear that the man had never heard of Ie Shima let alone the fact that there was an Air Force base there.

Vic and Bob sat in an air conditioned office with a rather harried man on the other side of the desk. He was confused as to where Vic and Bob had come from, what they were asking for, and why they were even in his office. There were constant interruptions of people barging in through the door with requests, problems, or questions that did little to help the poor man in focusing. By the end of the meeting, Vic and Bob were assured that a ferry system would be set up and operating within a week. The officer also promised that the radio requests would be honored and that the men would not be forgotten again.

Riding high on the promise of ferries and going home they

headed back to the airstrip in search of the plane that had carried them from their base. When they got to the airstrip they found the Piper Cub was gone. Someone else had "requisitioned" it and they were stranded in a completely new way. It took a bit of searching before Vic spotted a C-47 being loaded not far from where they had originally landed the Cub.

The pilot, a 1st lieutenant, was going through the preflight procedure with his co-pilot. They were about to take a load of supplies to Atsugi. Vic and Bob climbed into the cabin and approached the cockpit. Vic explained their predicament and asked if the pilot could drop them at Ie Shima. The pilot laughed and agreed.

After the foray into the chaos of the headquarters a launch called on Ie Shima regularly. It brought mail, beer, and medical supplies. Ferries started to arrive and carried men to the embarkation camp. By Christmas of 1945 every last man had been evacuated and was headed home. Vic himself returned to the States in a crowded troop ship in November. It was a demeaning way for an airman to travel, crammed into a troopship, packed in like canned fish alongside so many other military men, but it got them where they needed to be in the end.

Reflections After The War

During the fighting he lost many friends and he says you never really get used to it. He would sometimes see them go down; other times he just noticed, a few days after a mission that they were no longer around. It was surreal, but somehow it also didn't really make it in. He was too busy trying to survive himself that in those moments he had little room for grief or to mourn the fallen properly. It was just too big.

For Vic, he tended to focus more on the flying than on the planes being shot down around him. Flying and firing at the enemy was always an enjoyment to Vic even in the midst of the danger. It was a chance to get a shot of adrenaline, or hone his skills, or achieve a new goal. He never liked being shot at himself, and would have preferred that his targets simply refused to fire back and let him do his job. But war isn't won that way. He shot men down, and in return their fellows tried to tear him out of the sky. It was a hell of a thing, loving and hating where you are and what you're doing.

Vic had made it through the hell of war. He had seen men die, but too he had seen them live more completely than he ever would ever have otherwise. These men had formed bonds stronger than family, stronger than iron. They were forged in war and tempered with engine oil. So it was that Vic returned to the states a changed man. He was now a man of pride and strength of character that would carry him forward for many years. It is this power of will and courage of heart that caught and held the attention of those who met him along the way. It is this man, who fought and survived that terrible war, that I met one summer day and wondered what his story was. He shared it with me and I was compelled to record it. The end of the war was not merely the end of a story, but the beginning of a legacy of a truly great generation that will continue to live on in Vic's stories and others like them.

Campaign Ribbon or Award Medal	Authority	Order and Date
Asiatic & Pacific Ribbon	War Dept	Cir. 1 942
Philippine Liberation Ribbon	"	G.O. 23 5 Feb 1945
New Guinea Campaign	USAFF	G.O 18 24 Jan 1945
Southern Philippine Campaign	War Dept	G.O. 33 1 May 1945
Luzon Campaign	War Dept	G.O. 33 1 May 1945
Air Medal	5th AF	S.O. 340 30 May 1945
Oak Leaf Cluster - Air Medal	5th AF	S.O. 340 30 May 1945
Solomon Islands Campaign	War Dept	G.O. 101 8 Aug 1945
Bismark Archipelago Campaign	War Dept	G.O 100 28 Apr 1945
Western Pacific Campaign	AFPAC	G.O 128 28 Aug 1945
China Defensive Campaign	War Dept	G.O. 33 1 May 1945
Air Offensive - Japan	War Dept	G.O. 33 1 May 1945
2nd Oak Leaf Cluster - Air Medal	FEAF	G.O. 2180 9 Nov 1945
China Offensive Campaign	War Dept	G.O. 195 1945
American Campaign	War Dept	Cir 326 1945

Made in the USA
Charleston, SC
11 July 2015